ISLAM

اسلام

Text

Azra Kidwai

Photographs

Thomas L Kelly ❖ Kabir Khan

Taj Mohammad

ISLAM

Lustre Press

Roli Books

ISBN: 81-7436-056-5

© Roli Books Pvt. Ltd., 1998
  Lustre Press Pvt. Ltd.
Second impression 2002
M-75, Greater Kailash-II Market
New Delhi-1100048, India
Tel: (011) 6442271, 6462782; Fax: (011) 6467185
E-mail: roli@vsnl.com; Website: rolibooks.com

Text: Azra Kidwai
Concept and Design: Ranmal Singh Jhala
Produced at Roli CAD Centre

Photocredits :
Christine Pemberton (Fotomedia) : Page 65 (above)
Hemen Sanghvi : Pages 94-95
Kabir Khan : Pages 2-3, 11 (below), 18-19, 26, 33, 66
Marie D'Souza (Fotomedia) : Page 76 (right)
Pradeep Bose : Page 34
Ranmal Singh Jhala : Pages 1, 13,15, 16, 17, 21, 35,
41 (above), 65 (below), 69, 74 (below), 85 (below),
87 (below)
Sanjay Singh Badnor : Pages 89 (above), 90-91
Sondeep Shankar : Pages 4-5
Taj Mohammad : Pages 30-31, 37, 43, 44, 45 (above),
46-47, 48 (below), 60, 74 (above), 82, 86 (below), 88,
92, 93, 96
T C Jain (Fotomedia) : Page 56
Thomas L Kelly : Cover and backcover, Pages 6, 22, 38,
41, 45 (below), 48 (above), 52, 54, 57, 61, 64,
77 (below), 86 (middle)

Photo courtesy :
Azra Kidwai : Pages 32, 81
Embassy of Saudi Arabia : Page 11
Li Xiaoguo and Shen Qiao (Embassy of the People's
Republic of China) : Page 51
The Royal Embassy of Saudi Arabia : Page 11
Maharaja of Orchha : Page 17
Rampur Raza Library : Pages 28-29
Roli Books : Pages 40, 41 (below), 50, 58-59, 62, 67, 68,
70, 72, 73, 75, 76 (left), 77 (above), 78-79, 80, 85 (above
and below), 86 (above), 87 (above), 89 (below)

Map on Page 3 : Historical Atlas of the Muslim People
(Amsterdam, 1957), courtesy, Indian Institute of Islamic
Studies, Jamia Hamdard Library, Delhi, India.
Map on Pages 24-25 : Saurabh Mahendru

Printed and bound at
Star Standard Industries Pte Ltd
Singapore

*Namazis at the Fatehpuri
mosque in Delhi, India, for
jumma al-vida, the last Friday
prayer in the month of
Ramadan.*

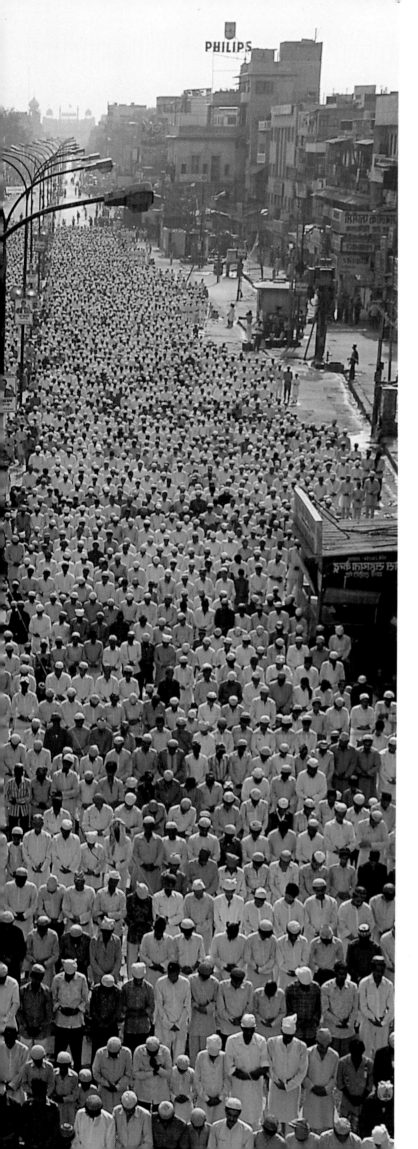

Contents

Bis-mi-Allah-e-Rahman-e-Rahim, *We begin in the name of God, the compassionate and the merciful; from on eighteenth century Afghan Quran.*

"Say ye: We believe
In God, and the revelation
Given to us, and to Abraham,
Ismail, Isaac, Jacob,
And the Tribes, and that given
To Moses and Jesus, and that given
To (all) Prophets from their Lord:
We make no difference
Between one and another of them:
And we bow to God (in Islam)."

Sura II, 136

Genesis

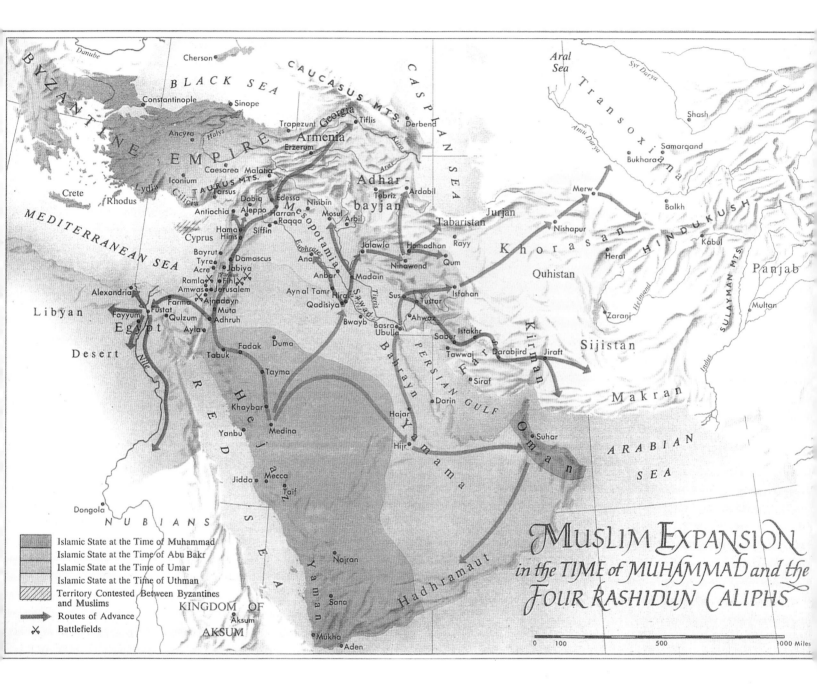

MUSLIM EXPANSION
in the TIME of MUHAMMAD and the FOUR RASHIDUN CALIPHS

Aral Sea

Syr Darya

BLACK SEA

CAUCASUS MTS.

CASPIAN SEA

Transoxiana

Amu Darya

Cherson

Constantinople · Sinope

BYZANTINE EMPIRE

Ancyra

Halys

Trapezunt Georgia · Tiflis · Derbend

Erzerum

Caesarea Malatia

Iconium

Cilicia TAURUS MTS.

Tarsus

Antiochia Aleppo Harran

Dabia Edessa Nisibin

Armenia

Adhar-bayjan

Tebriz · Ardabil

Jurjan

Shash

Samarqand

Bukhara

Balkh

HINDUKUSH

Merw

Nishapur

Khorasan

Kabul

Panjab

MEDITERRANEAN SEA

Cyprus

Hama Hims Siffin

Mesopotamia Mosul · Arbil

Raqqa

Euphrates

Mardin

Bayrut Damascus

Tyre Jabiya

Acre Yarmuk

Ramla Fihl

Amwas Ajnadayn Jerusalem

Ana

Anbar

Madain

Jalawla

Homadhan

Nihawend

Qum

Rayy

Tabaristan

Herat

Quhistan

Alexandria

Fayyum

Fustat

Qulzum

Ayla

Egypt

Adhruh

Muta

Ayn al Tamr Hira

Qadisiya

Sawad

Tigris

Sus Tustar

Bwayb

Basra

Ubulla

Ahwaz

Sabur

Isfahan

Zaranj

Multan

SULAYMAN MTS.

Indus

Sijistan

Libyan Desert

Nile

RED SEA

Hejaz

Fadak Duma

Tabuk

Tayma

Khaybar

Yanbu Medina

Bahrayn

Hajar

Hijr

Darin

PERSIAN GULF

Siraf

Istakhr

Tawwaj

Darabjird Jiraft

Fars

Kirman

Makran

Oman Suhar

ARABIAN SEA

NUBIANS

Dongola

Jidda · Mecca

Taif

Najran

Yaman

Sana

Mukha

Aden

Hadhramaut

KINGDOM OF AKSUM

Aksum

Yamama

Islamic State at the Time of Muhammad
Islamic State at the Time of Abu Bakr
Islamic State at the Time of Umar
Islamic State at the Time of Uthman
Territory Contested Between Byzantines and Muslims
Routes of Advance
Battlefields

0   100   500   1000 Miles

The Arabian peninsula where Islam first appeared lay at the edge of two great and ancient civilisations: the Egyptian and the Mesopotamian. Both these civilisations were irrigated by mighty rivers, the Nile and Tigris respectively. Arabia on the other hand had no rivers and thus very little cultivation. The development and prosperity in the neighbouring worlds seemed to pass it by.

Closer to the time of Muhammad's birth, the peninsula was on the margins of two other powerful empires: the Byzantine and the Sassanian. The Byzantine Empire with its capital at Constantinople (modern Istanbul) was concentrated around the Mediterranean Sea and included the Anatolian and Balkan peninsulas, Syria and Egypt. The Sassanian Empire had its capital at Ctesiphon (close to modern Baghdad) and included Iraq and Iran and extended right up to the river Indus. Both empires controlled vast, fertile lands, busy trade routes and had large armies and bureaucracies.

The two empires also had a close relationship between state and religion. Christianity was the official religion of the Byzantine Empire and Zoroastrianism was widespread among the Sassanians. The religious traditions of this wider region were an important backdrop for the rise of Islam. This area had seen the appearance of universal monotheistic religions which demanded the individual's adherence to a cosmological belief system and belonged to two main traditions:

- ❖ The Abrahamic tradition of the Hebrew prophets of which Judaism and Christianity are the examples.
- ❖ The Magian tradition of which Zoroastrianism is the most important.

Both these monotheistic groups believed in the prophetic tradition, a universal scripture and one transcendental god. They also believed that human beings had just one life and that there was life after death. Whether this life was going to be spent in Heaven or Hell depended on one's actions. They advocated a life of individual moral responsibility because man was accountable to god for his deeds.

The power of Islam grew rapidly after the death of Usman and made inroads into the mighty Byzantine and Sassanian empires as shown in the map.

The Byzantine and Sassanian empires competed with each other for resources and territories but they largely ignored the Arabian peninsula. It is not difficult to see why. Most parts of the peninsula were dry, barren and often inaccessible except on camels. The landscape consisted mostly of sandy deserts, arid steppes and an occasional oasis. The climate too was extremely inhospitable. The two empires also realised that controlling the nomadic tribes which lived in Arabia would be very difficult and definitely not worth losing men and money over. It was easier to deal with them by hiring them or paying them off.

The dry Arabian sands were inhabited by various tribes called the Bedouins. Each tribe consisted of a number of clans claiming common ancestry. The tribe therefore considered itself a distinct entity, tied by blood and willing to fight for its interests and avenge any wrong done to its members.

Some of these tribes had settled in areas which were well watered and allowed for regular cultivation of dates and wheat. Others continued to be nomadic, constantly moving with their livestock in search of food and water. Since natural resources were scarce and pasture lands had to be fought for, inter-tribal warfare was an integral part of Bedouin life. This state of constant tension was sharpened by the tribal belief in blood feud. Every death had to be avenged by the tribe. This endless cycle of violence made political unity within Arabia impossible.

Despite these animosities, there were cultural traditions that were common to the Bedouins. They were united by a common language—Arabic, a rich literary tradition and a sense of common history. Each tribe had its own idols, trees, rocks and spirits that it worshipped but the Ka'ba (*haram*), the holy sanctuary at Mecca, was revered by many of the tribes. The Arabs also worshipped a powerful though vague figure called Allah, the supreme god regarded as the Creator.

The Bedouin society was like any other nomadic group. There were no rich and poor within a tribe, all were equal. Nomadic life reinforced this relative equality for people could only possess as much as they could comfortably travel with. Tribal values were based on hereditary economic and social

An engraving showing a Zoroastrian Parsee priest reciting a religious text while tending a temple fire. Zoroastrianism was the state religion of the Sassanian empire which was rapidly incorporated into Islam.

solidarity expressed through shared responsibilities and resources in good times and bad.

The Bedouin society was a tri-level pyramidical structure. At the base was the family; related families together formed clans and a number of such clans came together to form tribes. Each tribe was headed by a Saiyyid, chosen not because of his descent but because of his wisdom and courage. His decisions were morally binding on every member of the tribe. Since loyalties were based on clan and kinship ties, the Bedouin society rejected authoritarian political forms. Major decisions like war which involved the lives of all members of the tribe were taken by consensus. The Saiyyid did not nominate his successor, he was selected by consensus from among the various clans.

For their livelihood, the Bedouins depended on livestock, particularly camels, horses, goats and sheep. Camels were crucial to their lives for many reasons: their flesh and milk provided food, they could travel long distances (well over a hundred miles a day), carry heavy loads (over five hundred kilograms) and could do without food or water for eight days at a stretch. They could also survive in temperatures up to fifty seven degrees celsius.

No wonder the domestication of camels made the Bedouins an important social force. They could now not just defend themselves but also raid and extract tribute from the settled areas; they were a recruiting ground for mercenaries and most important, they became protectors of trade and trade routes. The economic resources of the tribes were supplemented by raiding the resources of other tribes and trade-caravans which moved under their protection.

In the sixth century particularly, political developments in the neighbouring lands made the Bedouins crucial to world trade. The constant warfare between the Byzantine and the Sassanian empires blocked the land routes from Asia to the Mediterranean lands and Europe. An alternative trade route was found across the Arabian peninsula. Textiles, spices and luxury foods from the East were brought by sea to the southern ports of the peninsula. From ports in Yemen they were transported

The Bedouins of Arabia were nomads who carried their homes—their tents—with them.

Above, left : *A symbolic picture depicting the date palm and the camel, both basic to the sustenance of the Arabs.*

Today the Arabs are a settled community but the camel remains a prized possession.

over land on camel-back to the Mediterranean ports. Similarly, goods from Africa, particularly slaves—who were in great demand—were shipped across the Red Sea and then conveyed over land to markets in Asia. Commerce and trading thus exposed the Arabs to the workings of big empires and the intricacies of world trade.

One direct result of this increased economic activity was the rise of the city of Mecca. Mecca did not have an oasis though it did have the spring Zam zam which provided drinking water to the city. It had no agriculture, it was in fact completely dependent on the import of food.

The importance of Mecca was however, the result of three factors: the north-south and the east-west trade routes across the peninsula intersected at Mecca and it developed into a bustling commercial centre. The Bedouins who had settled there learnt the complexities of international trade and soon became successful traders themselves.

Second, Mecca was where the holiest shrine of the Bedouins, the Ka'ba, was located. The annual pilgrimage by different tribes had developed into an important fair and brought plenty of business.

Third, and equally crucial, Mecca was controlled by the tribe of Quraysh, one of the largest tribes of Arabia.

The Quraysh had settled in Mecca and had been successful in organising the trade system within the peninsula to their advantage. They made alliances with other tribes and created what is often referred to as the 'Commonwealth of Mecca'. Their annual trade with Syria alone has been estimated as being worth about eleven thousand kilograms of gold.

The Quraysh were also the protectors of the Ka'ba, within which they had accommodated the gods of other tribes. They guaranteed the safety of those who came to worship here, particularly during *Hajj*, the annual pilgrimage. The Quraysh also ensured that there was no fighting during the four months that they had deemed sacred. They thus managed to maintain the peace that was so essential for trade and as a result flourished.

A Greek inscription from the third century AD.

A Syriac funerary inscription from 338 AD referring to Imrul-Qayas, a famous pre-Islamic poet.

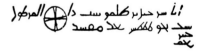

An Arabic inscription from 518 AD. Muslims contributed immensely to the development of the Arabic script, elevating it to the status of an art.

Abraham

In southern Iraq, once Mesopotamia, in the kingdom of Nimrod, was born Abraham. His people worshipped planets and idols made of wood and stone. Abraham's own father was an idol-maker but could not convince his son that his creations were worthy of worship. Abraham was not willing to pray to objects which were perishable.

When he grew a little older, Allah or God sent him messages through the angel Gabriel (Jibra'il) that there was only one God and that he, Abraham, had been chosen to spread this message to one and all.

But these words of God were ignored by Abraham's kinsmen, until one day Abraham went into the temple while the rest of his people were elsewhere and broke each idol there barring the biggest. The priest and the people were furious. Certain that no one other than Abraham could have been responsible for this blasphemy, they summoned him to the court and asked him to explain. Abraham in his defence suggested that the chief idol, still intact in the temple and which had witnessed the events, be asked to testify. Though Abraham had made his point, he was made to leave the town. He and his wife, Sara went to Palestine where he continued to preach God's message.

Since Abraham had no son, he married again and from his second wife Hajira, he had a son, Ismail, who grew up to be a Prophet himself. After the birth of Ismail, Abraham was ordered by God to go further and preach. It was a long and difficult journey, through barren hills and stony deserts particularly for Hajira and the infant Ismail. On one occasion Ismail began to wail due to thirst. His mother Hajira ran desperately from one hillock to another searching for water but in vain. She returned to find a stream emerging from under the heels of the infant. This spring is the Zam zam around which Mecca, the holy shrine of the Muslims developed later.

When Ismail was a young boy, Abraham in a dream was ordered by God to sacrifice his son. Without a moment's hesitation, on the tenth day of Dhul i Hijja, the last month of the Muslim calendar, he took Ismail to Mina, blindfolded himself and started the sacrifice. When he had finished and removed his blindfold, Abraham found that God had replaced his son with a ram.

Abraham was rewarded with another son, Ishaaq (Isaac), this time from his first wife, Sara. He was also ordered to build the Ka'ba, the House of God, at Mecca.

The Ka'ba continues to be the sanctified House of God for Muslims. Abraham's sacrifice is venerated with the annual pilgrimage to this abode of God that Abraham built. Abraham's sons too were Prophets. Ismail was a Muslim and an ancestor of Muhammad. The Jews are descendents of the second son, Ishaaq.

A calendar art picture of the Ka'ba, the most important shrine of Muslims, built by Abraham.

Muhammad

It was in the Banu Hashim clan of the Quraysh tribe that Muhammad was born in AD 570 in Mecca. His father Abdullah died before his birth and his mother Amina died when he was six. Muhammad was thus brought up by his grandfather and later by his uncle.

Like his fellow tribesmen, Muhammad too became a trader and was employed by Khadija, a wealthy merchant's widow. Though fifteen years older than him, Muhammad married her at the age of twenty-five. When he began to preach the word of God, Khadija was the first to believe him and his role as the Prophet. She befriended Muhammad, trusted him and understood his spiritual struggles.

The word of God was first revealed to Muhammad in a very personal experience. He used to often retreat to meditate in a cave in the mountains outside Mecca. On one such retreat, the arch-angel Gabriel appeared before Muhammad. Gripped in a trance, Muhammad became conscious of ideas which he did not recognise to be his own. 'The veil was lifted from the chosen one's eyes and his soul for a moment was filled by divine ecstasy.'

Muhammad shared this experience with his wife Khadija who believed it and rejoiced in it. She comforted him since he was physically distraught and shaken by the experience. She was convinced that it was not a dream or a delusion but that her husband was God's chosen one to renew the faith.

Gradually Muhammad realised that he was *Rasul Allah*, the Messenger of God. He continued to receive these messages till the time of his death.

In the beginning, as is stated in the Quran, these experiences were both auditory and ocular. The auditions were simple: Muhammad heard words or simple sounds, to which meanings were attached on his emergence from the trance. This message which he proclaimed to the world, a message of divine and sublime beauty, was a warning to the heedless, a guide to the erring, an assurance to those in doubt and solace to those suffering.

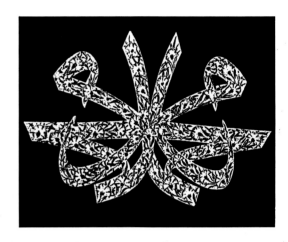

Mirror image of the Prophet's name transcribed by Turkish calligrapher Suhail Amar. Whenever Muslims utter the name of the Prophet, they reverently prefix it with Sallalaho Alai he Wasallum (Peace be unto Him).

The initial revelations stressed God's unity, the obligation to help the poor and the destitute and warned those who hoarded wealth and exploited the helpless of the impending Day of Judgement.

Muhammad's message questioned the basis on which life in Mecca was organised. He envisaged a community which was based on a common faith, not one based on ties of clan or tribe. In a society where social and economic differences had become entrenched, Muhammad advocated the equality of all before their creator, Allah. He stressed that it was to the creator and not to the tribe that men owed their survival. He insisted that individuals had the freedom to act and that they had to be responsible for their actions.

Though the message of Islam was for all humanity, it were the orphans, the poor, the slaves and the deprived who were first attracted to it. Muhammad spoke of the responsibility of the rich and powerful towards the less privileged; he spoke against usury and unfair economic practices. According to him, no one had the right to hoard if there were others in need.

The first believers of Muhammad were his wife Khadija, his friend and counsellor Abu Bakr, his ten year old cousin Ali and a slave called Zaid. Gradually, as Muhammad's word spread, an increasing number of people began believing in him. Early converts to Islam were drawn from three broad groups: members of weaker clans who were faced with hard times because of the increasing monopolisation of trade by a powerful few; junior members of powerful clans who were victims of inequality within their own clans and finally there were the slaves and 'clients' (*mawalis*). The 'clients' were associated with the tribes but were not members of any clan. Since it was the tribe which protected people and no one could exist without being formally a part of it, many who fell out with their tribes or were rendered defenceless because of war, entered into a patron-client relationship with other tribes. The tribe was responsible for the clients' protection but they were not considered equal members of the tribe. Since the Meccans were rich and powerful, the city had a large number of these clients and slaves.

The crescent moon, the emblem of the mighty Sassanian empire, is a popular Islamic symbol. Here, the Kalima or the Faith, Ya ilaha illallah Muhammad Rasul Allah (God is great and Muhammad is His Prophet) is framed within the crescent.

Those in control of Mecca did not like this voice of dissent from within. They began to get all the more alarmed when important and powerful Meccans who had first ridiculed Muhammad started converting to Islam. Initially, Muhammad's clan ties protected him from open persecution. Besides, he could take refuge with his uncle Abu Talib, head of the Banu Hashim clan. But after his uncle's death in AD 619, the next head of the clan refused to protect Muhammad for fear of economic boycott.

Muhammad turned to Allah for guidance who advised that the Muslims migrate from Mecca. On 24 September, AD 622, Muhammad and his followers began their journey to Medina, then called Yathrib, two hundred and eighty kilometers north of Mecca. This journey called *hijra* is of tremendous significance to the Muslims for it is the occasion when they abandoned their old clan and tribal links to live in a community with other Muslims, irrespective of clan, tribe or race. It was the formal establishment of the *ummah*—the Muslim community. Even today the *Hijri* or the Muslim calendar, a lunar one, begins from this day.

Masjid-e-Nabi, the Prophet's mosque at Medina. Though a visit to Medina is not an essential ritual of the Hajj, it has become a tradition for pilgrims to pay their obeisance here at the grave of their religion's founder.

Unlike Mecca which was a bustling commercial centre, Medina was an agricultural settlement around an oasis. The tribal groups and Jewish settlements who inhabited this oasis welcomed the Muslims, for Medina at this time was faced with a complete breakdown of political order. Inter-group warfare had disrupted life. There were major conflicts among the residents and disputes over blood, money and revenge had not been resolved. Muhammad's reputation as the wise one preceded him and various groups in Medina invited him to fill in the traditional role of the arbitrator (*hakam*) and restore peace. But Muhammad's authority was only nominal since he had no force to back it. Yet, by being asked to play peacemaker, Muhammad was now assigned a political role. He also made the first converts to Islam outside Mecca from among the Medinians and the community soon began to grow through conversions.

At the time of migration, a formal document of agreement was worked out between Muhammad and the residents of Medina. This document called the *Constitution of Medina* survives to this day. It envisaged the settlement of Medina as one political entity, a single community comprising three main groups: the emigrants or *muhajirun*, the *ansars* or hosts at Medina and the Jews as a protected religious group.

The Muslims at Medina first prayed facing Jerusalem, a city sacred to the Jews, Christians and Muslims. Later, the Quran instructed the Muslims to face Mecca when they said their prayers.

Once settled in Medina, the Meccan Muslims could not become agriculturists like the other settlers. Since they had come from a trading community, it was to this that they turned. They challenged the Meccan trade system by harassing the caravans going

Overleaf : The Dome of the Rock built by Khalil Abdal Malik (685-705 AD) to celebrate the victory of Islam over the Byzantine and Sassanian empires. Built above the Sakkra rock, the highest point of Mount Mariah, the plan around the canopied shrine follows the pre-Islamic tradition.

An Afghan carpet showing the winged steed Ul Burraq. Muslims believe that Ul Burraq is the divine beast on which Muhammad made his celestial trip. It has a human face, horse's mane, camel's legs, cow's body and a chest and tail of rubies.

to and coming from Syria. They also disrupted the food supply to Mecca. By AD 624, the Muslims had gained important victories. They won enormous booty, four-fifths of which was declared as public property and distributed among all Muslims. One-fifth was the leader's share which Muhammad used for managing the affairs of the community. These victories demonstrated the exceptional military skills of Muhammad. They also added to his prestige for they confirmed the truth of Muhammad's vision.

However, as the peninsular trade was controlled by the Quraysh, conflict with the Meccans was unavoidable. In AD 625, the Meccans launched a campaign against the Muslims, aimed at destroying Muhammad's power. But the mighty army of three thousand men and two hundred cavalry was routed by a small but spirited Muslim force.

A successive, more forceful attempt by the Meccans to vanquish the Muslims also failed. With the increasing success of Islam, more and more tribes were attracted to Muhammad and his followers. As the community grew, it became clear to Muhammad that peace was essential for the prosperity of his people as continuing conflict was bound to destroy trade throughout the Arabian peninsula. He therefore initiated a move towards reconciliation by declaring his desire to perform the *Hajj* (pilgrimage).

In AD 630, a truce was arranged. The Meccans submitted and allowed the Muslims to enter the city. The Muslims in turn did not treat Mecca as war booty and left it untouched. Muhammad also pointedly established that his religion held the Ka'ba in the greatest esteem. His *Hajj* also included many pre-Islamic rituals.

Following the *Hajj*, the Meccans were accepted into the *ummah* or the Muslim community. After taking Mecca, Muhammad insisted on conversion for those wanting to join him. But this did not stop him from making alliances with tribes, particularly the more distant ones, with no religious preconditions. God constantly guided the young community through Muhammad. His word was the religious truth. Thus,

after the fall of Mecca, Muhammad came to possess supreme political and religious authority within the *ummah*. He was the undisputed leader.

Most Medinans converted to Islam when Muhammad returned from Mecca. The few Jews and Christians who continued to live in Medina were given the status of *zimmis* or protected people. The *ummah* of Medina was a heterogenous group comprising people from different tribes united no longer by blood but by a common faith. The tribe was superseded as a system of bonding when Muhammad provided the supra-tribal ideal of the *ummah*.

The Arabs till now had lived off each other. Once Muhammad had established a new community and ensured peace within Arabia, new sources of income had to be found. So in his last years Muhammad concentrated on securing trade routes to Iraq and Syria. He died in AD 624 in his favourite wife Ayesha's chamber. His grave is now a part of the mosque complex built at that spot.

An aerial view of Muslims praying during Hajj. Muslim congregational prayers are usually performed in straight lines facing the Ka'ba. Here the congregation forms a concentric circle since it is gathered around the shrine.

How many of the Prophets
Fought (in God's way),
And with them (fought)
Large bands of godly men?
But they never lost heart
If they met with disaster
In God's way, nor did
They weaken (in will)
Nor give in, And God
Loves those who are
Firm and steadfast.

Sura III, 146

Bismillah *from the remarkable twelve volume Quran composed by al-Qaudusi in 1849.*

Expansion

1. AFGHANISTAN
2. ALBANIA
3. ALGERIA
4. ARGENTINA
5. ARMENIA
6. AUSTRALIA
7. AZARBAYJAN
8. BANGLADESH
9. BENIN
10. BOSNIA HERZEGOVINA
11. BRUNEI
12. BULGARIA
13. BURKINA FASO
14. CAMEROON
15. CANADA
16. CHAD
17. CHINA
18. CYPRUS
19. EGYPT
20. ERITREA
21. ETHIOPIA

22. FRANCE
23. GAMBIA
24. GEORGIA
25. GERMANY
26. GHANA
27. GREECE
28. GUINEA
29. GUINEA BISSAU
30. GUYANA
31. INDIA
32. INDONESIA
33. IRAN
34. IRAQ
35. ISRAEL
36. ITALY
37. IVORY COAST
38. JORDAN
39. KAZAKHSTAN
40. KENYA
41. KIRGHIZSTAN
42. KUWAIT

43. LEBANON
44. LIBERIA
45. LIBYA
46. MADAGASCAR
47. MALAWI
48. MALAYSIA
49. MALI
50. MAURITANIA
51. MONGOLIA
52. MOROCCO
53. MOZAMBIQUE
54. NEPAL
55. NIGER
56. NIGERIA
57. OMAN
58. PAKISTAN
59. PAPUA NEW GUINEA
60. POLAND
61. QATAR
62. RUSSIAN FEDERATION
63. SAUDI ARABIA

64. SENEGAL
65. SIERRA LEONE
66. SOMALIA
67. SPAIN
68. SUDAN
69. SURINAM
70. SYRIA
71. TAJIKISTAN
72. TANZANIA
73. TUNISIA
74. TURKEY
75. TURKMENISTAN
76. UGANDA
77. UKRAINE
78. UNITED ARAB EMIRATES
79. UNITED KINGDOM
80. UNITED STATES OF AMERICA
81. UZBEKISTAN
82. WESTERN SAHARA
83. YEMEN
84. YUGOSLAVIA

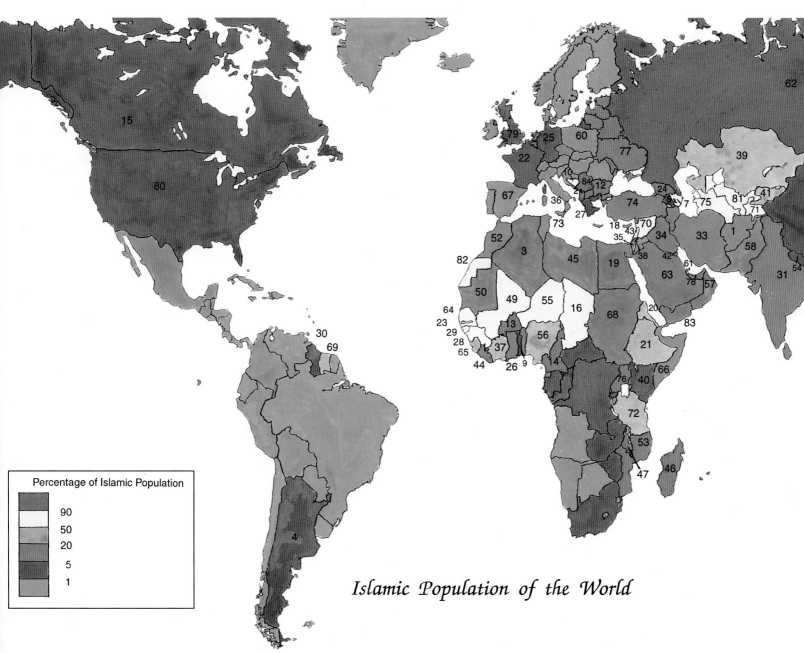

Percentage of Islamic Population

90
50
20
5
1

Islamic Population of the World

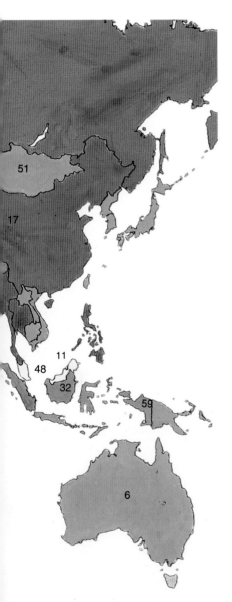

After Muhammad, the Muslim community was headed by a *khalifa* or caliph (viceroy) who exercised power on behalf of the Prophet. Naturally, he was not expected to take over the mantle of the Prophet, but given that the community was based on a common religion, the leader was bound to have both religious and temporal roles. The caliphs were therefore called *Khalifat ar Rasul*, Viceroys of the Prophet. The first four caliphs were from among the companions of Muhammad and were called the 'Rightly Guided Caliphs'.

The first of them was Abu Bakr, a friend of the Prophet's and the father of his wife Ayesha. During his short tenure (AD 632-34) he was mostly involved in establishing the political and religious authority of Medina over the rest of Arabia. This was essential because the tribal alliances forged by Muhammad had begun disintegrating after his death. Abu Bakr's hectic military activity ensured that even those tribes which had not been a part of the alliance during Muhammad's lifetime, now accepted the leadership of Medina. The mighty Sassanian and Byzantine forces were defeated in Iraq and in Syria, marking the beginning of the expansion of Islam outside the peninsula.

The next caliph, Umar, (AD 634-644 AD) continued the expansion. Damascus, Ctesiphon, Jerusalem, Alexandria and Mosul were taken by Muslim armies. Most of the fertile crescent, Egypt and Iran were now ruled by Muslim Bedouins. The mighty empires which prided themselves as being invincible were vanquished by this new movement that had emerged from Arabia.

Umar was a man of tremendous energy and administrative talents and laid the foundations for the future institutions of the Islamic regime. He did not disturb the life of the newly conquered areas. The existing economic and social structures including law and religion were allowed to continue—only the rulers were replaced. Most significantly, Umar forbade his troops from settling on the land. This policy was of great importance for it did not let the momentum of expansion dissipate. Only moveable wealth gained in battle and taxes were

appropriated by the new regime, four-fifths of which was distributed within the community.

Umar did not make any converts. Non-Muslims were given the status of *zimmis* and had to pay the land tax as well as a tax on each adult individual—the *jaziya*. In return, they did not have to join the armies of their conquerors. Umar created new encampments to garrison the troops, thus ensuring that the armies were separated from the people of the conquered areas. These encampments soon grew into major cities like Basrah, Kufah and Cairo.

Even on his deathbed Umar did not give up his efforts to organise the Islamic empire. As a parting act, he nominated a council to decide on a successor which elected Usman (AD 644-656). Under him, expansion in Iran and Egypt continued. However, Usman's choice of governors was criticised by many Muslims who felt that power was being monopolised by one family. A particularly controversial appointment was that of Muawiyyah, a cousin of Usman, as the governor of Syria.

To ensure doctrinal uniformity within the community, Usman ordered the standardisation of the Quran. This angered a very vocal group of people called the Qurra—the people who recited the Quran from memory. God's revelations to Muhammad had been memorised by many of his earlier followers and some of it had been written on different materials like the shoulder blades of camels, papyrii and so on.

The Qurra were held in great esteem because they were often the people's only access to the Quran. So when Usman ordered the suppression of all but the official version, the Qurra whose renderings differed were outraged and protested.

Among the opponents of Usman was Ali, the cousin and son-in-law of Muhammad. When Usman was murdered by a group of disgruntled Muslims in Medina, Ali seized the opportunity and declared himself caliph. (AD 656-61). The first civil war amongst Muslims broke out. Ayesha, the Prophet's widow, played a part in it. Many Muslims, including some companions of the Prophet were killed in this war. Sorrow reigned as in the aftermath of any war.

Facing Page : One of the holiest shrine of Shia Muslims, the mausoleum of Hazrat Massoumeh in Qum, Iran.

Overleaf : Pages from the Quran inscribed in the simplest Kufic script. The ornamental work in the margins are a later addition.

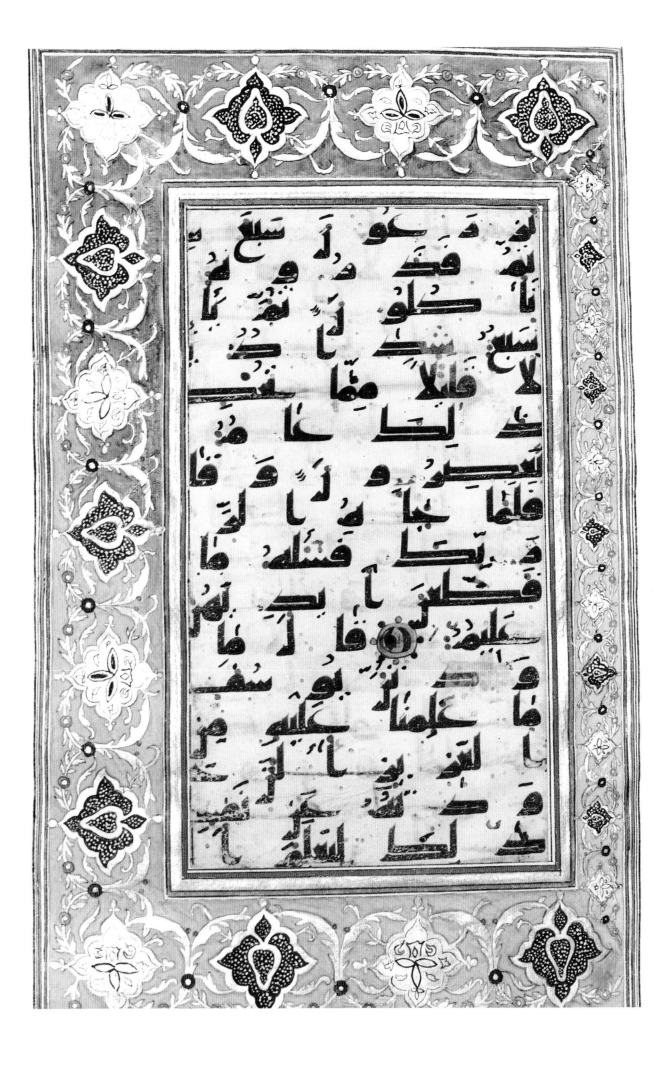

For many Muslims, Ali had a very special religious place. He had been among the first to accept Islam and was closely associated with the Prophet. He was brave, pious and idealistic. He was also the Prophet's cousin and the father of his only grandson. He had been a claimant for the caliphate since the death of Muhammad. A growing number of people came to support his cause and this group came to be called the Shi'at ul Ali—the party of Ali. The extremists among them attributed divine powers to Ali and out of religious conviction, they backed him against Muawiyyah; who was to establish the Umayyad caliphate after the death of Ali.

Umayyads

Muawiyyah (AD 661-680) declared himself caliph at Damascus. With the resources of Syria at his disposal and by appealing to the cause of Islamic unity, he garnered support from most of the community and reasserted the authority of the caliphate. Muawiyyah also resumed the process of expansion which had been halted in the past few years. The caliph's armies moved into eastern Iran and the Oxus valley; North Africa was conquered as far as Algeria. However, when he nominated his son Yazid as successor, the community was thrown into turmoil.

Above : Believers flagellating themselves during Muharram to remember the sufferings of Muslims at Karbala.

Below : Ya Abbas inscribed on a black bandana to commemorate Abbas (the grandson of Ali).

30

Though Yazid assumed authority as caliph (AD 680-685), civil war reappeared amongst the Muslims as the people of Medina refused to accept the principle of dynastic succession. The supporters of Ali (the Shias) set up their own regime at Kufah and gave the non-Arab Muslims (the *mawalis*) a share of the war booty. They also encouraged Husayn, the son of Ali and the grandson of Muhammad, to stake his claim to the caliphate. Husayn could only raise a very small force and refused to surrender when confronted with the superior armies of Yazid. He and his followers were massacred in AD 680 at Karbala.

As a warning to other rebels, Yazid had the severed head of Husayn displayed publicly. The slaughter of one of Muhammad's kin had a traumatic effect on the community. Resistance against Yazid became widespread in Arabia. His son and the next caliph Abdal Malik (AD 685-705) crushed the Medinan resistance and in the process of re-establishing the authority of the calpih, the Ka'ba was damaged. Abdal Malik's efforts to maintain the political unity of the Muslims was accompanied by state investment in irrigation and economic development. A uniform way of reciting the Quran was imposed and judges (*qazis*) were appointed in various garrison towns to settle disputes among Muslims. He also introduced new coins depicting Islamic legends.

Above & Below : A Majlis session during Muharram where moving accounts of the massacre at Karbala are being narrated. A highly developed art of oration, these renderings often leave the listeners in tears.

In the reign of the next caliph al Walid (AD 705-15), the expansion of the caliphate began again. The Berbers of North Africa who had converted to Islam now formed the vanguard of expansion into Europe. Spain was invaded in AD 711 and within a couple of years the entire country had been taken. The Arabs gave it a new name, Andalusia, and the Moorish culture—an amalgam of Arab-Spanish-Berber elements—grew out of this conquest.

In the east, the caliph's armies pushed into Sindh where the mercantile classes seem to have converted. In Central Asia, the caliphate expanded till it shared boundaries with China. Administrative unity was enforced by centrally appointed governors.

The caliphs had succeeded largely because they kept direct control over the economic resources of the empire. They abolished the tax privileges of the former elites and imposed a more equitable tax system which was widely welcomed. They did not interfere in the religious affairs of the conquered people and by removing discrimination against religious minorities in these areas, they ensured further support for themselves.

There were, however, groups that were severely at odds with the Umayyads, particularly in Iran where the Umayyad domination of the western lands was greatly resented. These groups joined forces under the banner of the Abbasids, the descendents of Abbas, a cousin of the Prophet. Supported by the Shias, they successfully challenged the Umayyads and in AD 750, Abu'l Abbas was proclaimed the first Abbasid caliph.

Two coins from Moorish Spain. Left: A gold dinar of Abd al-Mu'min (1130-63 AD), an Almohad caliph; Right: a fifteenth century silver dirham from the Kingdom of Granada.

Facing Page : *The famous Court of Lions, Alhambra Palace in Granada.*

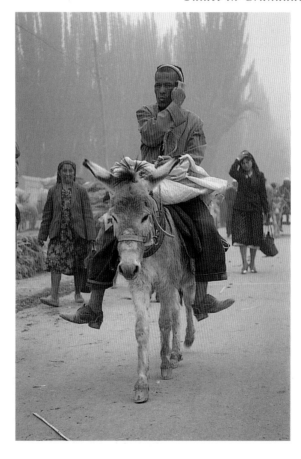

A traveller riding along the road in Kashgar, China, once a part of the famous Silk Route.

The facade and gateway of the mausoleum of caliph Ali ar-Rida, Prophet Muhammad's son-in-law, in Najaf, Iraq. Built in the late ninth or early tenth centuries, it is among the oldest surviving tombs of the Islamic world. Revered by all Muslims, it is an important place of pilgrimage, especially for the Shias.

Abbasids

The victory of the Abbasids can be seen as the culmination of the historical conflict between the provinces of Syria and Iraq. When the victorious Abbasids decided to build their new capital at Baghdad, it signified the end of the dominance of Syria over the affairs of the caliphate. It also signified the recognition of the power of the non-Arab Muslims.

The Abbasids were successful in routing the Umayyads because they espoused more popular causes. They tried to end the discrimination between Arabs and new Muslims. They inducted new groups into the ruling elite and this heterogenous ruling class they tried to unite by encouraging the evolution of a court-generated 'high culture'. They won over the critical, antagonistic religious groups by becoming patrons of Islamic learning, jurisprudence and theology. The Abbasids also involved the *ulama*, the Muslim learned men, in formulating and then disseminating cultural and religious traditions applicable to all Muslims. Baghdad, unlike early Islamic cities, was not organised on a tribal basis, thus reducing the role of tribes in the politics of the caliphate.

The Abbasids moved far ahead of the Umayyads in structuring the absolutist state. They adopted the court etiquette of the Sassanians and like them, projected themselves as semi-divine. Titles like 'Shadow of God on Earth' were adopted and courtiers were encouraged to kiss the ground in front of the caliph. The caliphs also started dispensing summary and unchallengeable justice. Opposition was dealt with with great severity. An elaborate bureaucracy and effective espionage system strengthened their hold over the empire. Financial matters were entrusted to a trustworthy noble. This responsibility was to evolve into the permanent office of the *wazir*, the all-powerful minister of subsequent Muslim empires. The Abbasids also invested in improving agricultural productivity and followed commercial policies which were an incentive for trade.

Harun al Rashid (AD 785-809) was the most well-known of the Abbasid caliphs. His rule is identified with splendour and grandeur and many believe that it is his reign that provided the background for the *Arabian Nights*. With the transfer of the capital from Syria to Iraq, the city of Baghdad was adopted as the imperial capital and there emerged a new cosmopolitan ruling group of Muslims of many races with Arabic as their medium of communication and Islam as their common bond and mark of identity. Harun al Rashid ran an efficient state managed by trained bureaucrats but it is his role as patron of the arts that brought him most fame. He encouraged artists, poets and musicians and rewarded them liberally. The aristocracy followed his example and Baghdad soon became a flourishing cultural and intellectual centre. Sciences and metaphysics were studied, the technique of paper-making was imported from China and soon paper replaced papyrus. Books on astronomy, medicine and mathematics were translated into Arabic from Greek and Sanskrit. Needless to say it was the flourishing economy of the caliphate that made much of this possible. The economy in turn prospered because of the comparative peace and the huge size of the empire. Banking, credit and postal services developed, towns increasingly became the hub of intense commercial activity. One indirect result of the economic developments in the history of Islam was that the religion won new adherents. Many who flocked to the towns found it convenient to convert. This led to the development of a more populist form of Islam in which the new converts carried their old traditions. This Islam was free from theological debates and was more a way of life than a dogma.

Harun however made an utopian decision which spelt trouble for the caliphate. He decided to partition his empire among his three sons at the time of death. The inevitable civil war resulted which almost wrecked the state structure. Al Mamun who had been given the eastern region eventually laid siege to Baghdad. The city rose in rebellion. Other governors like the Aghlabids in North Africa and Tahirids in Khurasan started assuming autonomous roles.

A scene from 'A Thousand and One Nights', better known as the 'Arabian Nights'. This famous collection of stories was compiled in the reign of Harun al Rashid (785-809 AD).

Al Mu'tasim (AD 833-44) realised how dependent the caliphs had become on the governors and their armies and decided to raise a personal force which would be loyal only to him. He started purchasing young slaves to be trained as soldiers, most of them Turks from the northern part of the empire. Since these slaves had no links with the local population, they were far easier to control. Al Mu'tasim also freed himself from the pressure groups at Baghdad by shifting his capital. The caliphs thus ensured their safety but at the cost of distancing themselves from the bureaucracy and other instruments of state.

The increasing dependence on slaves made the caliphs vulnerable to this new force that they themselves had created. They had pampered these troops, but with declining income, growing corruption and civil disaffection, the slave-troops started asserting their power over the caliph. The caliphs tried to mend the situation by introducing other ethnic elements into the soldiery and playing off one group against the other. This deliberate creation of factional strife within the most powerful group rebounded on them—they became pawns in the struggle for power.

By the tenth century, the caliphs had surrendered power to their Turkish generals. The caliphate however began to crumble as independent kingdoms sprang up in different regions. The Aghlabids and then Fatimids in Tunisia, the Fatimids in Egypt, the Zaydi Shias in Yemen, the Hamdanis in Mosul and the Samanids in north eastern Iran became independent of the caliphate. Eventually in AD 945, the Buyids from the area south of the Caspian Sea invaded Baghdad and made the caliph their puppet. The caliph survived but the caliphate became a myth.

The appearance of independent Muslim states introduced an interesting dichotomy in the Muslim mind. Muslims were one *ummah* and yet had to live in different states. This contradiction was seized and Islam developed differently in different parts of the world. Yet developments were never isolated to one area because, given the cultural links, contacts between Muslims were never disrupted.

Two warriors of eleventh century Fatimid Egypt carrying spears. The one on the left also has a sword (sayf) and a two-horned helmet.

Development of the Ummah

The idea of all Muslims being a part of one community—the 'ummah'—is basic to Islam. The 'ummah' was to live its life in accordance with the same norms of generosity, humility, patience and mercifulness as the Prophet. It was to be motivated by the same desire—to be truly obedient to Allah. Its scripture was the word of God, eternal and inalterable, and it lay down the fundamental duties of every Muslim. All Muslims are governed by the same laws.

The Shias believed in the divinely guided 'imam' as their leader. They felt that the link between God and Muslims had not ended with the death of the Prophet. As long as Ali was alive he was considered the 'imam'. After him, the Shias believed that there would be a series of others. Since the 'imams', were descendents of the Prophet through his daughter Fatima and her husband Ali, they were supposed to have special religious insight. As time passed, conflicts over the line of legitimate successors to the 'imamate' led to three splits within the Shias. Each group insisted that the 'imamate' came to an end with one specific 'imam' though they all believed that the last 'imam' had not died but had concealed himself ('ghayba') and would emerge at a specific time. Based on the number of 'imams' they believe in, the Shias are divided into the Twelvers, the Seveners and the Fivers. The Twelvers (Ithna Asharis) are by far the largest group among the Shias and also the least politically active.

The community was however, not left without guidance in the 'imam's' absence. The concealed 'imam' continued to guide the believers through signs sent to his special agents.

Thus, inspite of the original conception of the 'ummah' as one religio-political community, there emerged rifts that forced the Muslims to live in different political communities. Once such political entities were established independent of the caliphate, Muslim social theorists set about redefining the idea of the 'ummah'. They began emphasising the religious rather than the political unity of the Muslims and that they continued to be one 'ummah' even if they lived in different warring states. The concept of community had thus come a long way from its original definition.

The Ummah and Non-Muslims

The Muslims early in their history had to define their attitude towards the non-Muslims. The early and rapid spread of Islam brought them into contact with non-Muslims belonging to various religions. The pragmatism that was central to Islam as a religion was displayed here too. The Quran makes distinction between two categories of non-Muslims:

❖ The 'ahl i kitab' or the people of the book. These were religions which had their own revealed scriptures.
❖ The Pagans.

The Quran specifically mentions the Jews and Christians as people of the book. They were to be protected if they paid the poll-tax and accepted the political authority of the Muslims.

Muslims however stretched this category to include other religious groups as well. They used the assertion of the Quran that Allah had sent prophets and books to all people to justify the inclusion. The 'ahl i kitab' were free to practice their religions and their protection was one of the duties of the Muslims. The non-Muslims were thus categorised as the protected people.

Caps sold outside a mosque for men to cover their heads during namaaz (prayer).

بسم الله الرحمن الرحيم

Overturn your speech and utterance,
Keep vain imaginings away.
Walk not in the movements
Of Before and After.
And pass through the desert
Of human order and institutions.
Wander as though mad with love
Among those who are distracted by love
And grasp the upward-leading sense
That you may become a bird flying
Between mountains and hills;
Mountains of intellectuality,
And hills of self-esteem,
In order that you may see what is there
And that you may become the sword
Of the one who strikes in the secret mosque.

Al Hallaj

Customs and Beliefs

Islam means submission to the will of Allah: The One and Only God who is the Compassionate and the Merciful. He has created the universe and continues to guide the community. This guidance is contained in his message to humanity that He has periodically revealed through various Prophets, like Moses and Jesus, each of whom is identified with a revealed book (the Torah and the Gospel). Muhammad is considered the last and greatest of all the Prophets; and his Quran supersedes all previous books of revelation and is considered the final word of God.

Men reading the Quran inside a mosque.

Mankind was one single nation
And God sent Messengers
With glad tidings and warnings;
And with them He sent
The Book in truth,
To judge between people
in matters wherein
They differed;

God by his Grace
Guided the Believers
To the Truth,
Concerning that wherein they differed.
For God guides
Whom He will
To a path
That is straight.

Sura II 2

Facing Page: Eid prayers at Delhi's Jama Masjid (Friday Mosque), built by the Mughal emperor Shah Jahan in the seventeenth century. Even today, the faithful throng to this historic mosque on Eid day, filling the courtyard and spilling onto the streets.

Muslims recognise all Prophets from Adam onwards as Allah's messengers. Moses and Christ were the Prophets who preceded Muhammad; Abraham, the man willing to sacrifice his son to prove his obediance and love for God, is considered the first Muslim. Islam is thus the last phase in the long process of development of monotheistic religions like Judaism and Christianity.

41

The same religion has He
Established for you as that
Which he enjoined on Noah—
The which we have sent
By Inspirations to thee—
And that which was enjoined
On Abraham, Moses and Jesus.

Sura XLII 42

Muslims believe that Muhammad is the last Prophet (*rasul*), the 'Seal of the Prophets'. No other Prophets will follow him and the Quran is the last of God's message to humanity. This message was revealed to Muhammad by God himself. Muhammad recited these verses to his slowly growing audience, many of whom memorised them. These were compiled into the Quran after his death.

The word Quran means reading or recitation. It embodies the word of God, the core of which is inscribed on a tablet in heaven. The Quran comprises 114 chapters called *suras* (steps of unequal size), arranged in order of length. Each *sura* consists of a number of *ayats* which form the actual units of the Quran. The book is divided into 30 equal parts called *juz* in Arabic. In Persian and Urdu, they are called *sipara* or simply *para*.

Reading the Quran is not just the duty of every faithful Muslim but also a way of worshipping God. To recite it is to affirm one's faith in Him and it is through reading it that man can finally arrive at the knowledge of God.

The Quran conveys Allah's message in beautiful, lyrical Arabic that no translation has yet done justice to. Simple analogies and well-known historical references are used to underline God's unity: God is the creator of all, He created Adam and therefore all humanity. The Quran is meant to guide the believers, to make them believe in Him and submit to His will, to worship and believe in His kindness and His justice. The Quran prescribes duties for all Muslims and forbids certain things. It in fact lays down the basic guidelines for the individual and the norms for society.

Though the Quran does not forbid women from joining the men in offering prayers at the mosque, most women prefer to remember God by reading the Quran, at home or in the mosque.

The five precepts of Islam denoted by an open hand.

Facing Page, above : *Namaaz being offered by a congregation.*

Facing Page, below : *A man holding prayer beads.*

Devotees performing wuzu before namaaz.

But Islam acknowledges that humans have wills of their own and that they must make their own choices. However, it also reminds them of the Day of Judgement, the day of reckoning when the good will be rewarded with a life in heaven while the sinners have to pay for their trespasses in hell.

The Quran imposes five essential duties or *farz* on Muslims. Often referred to as the 'five pillars of the faith', these are:

Faith or *Kalima* : 'There is no God but Allah and Muhammad is his Prophet.' Recitation and belief in this declaration is essential for every Muslim. Muslims also believe that this proclamation allows a person entry into Islam.

Prayers or *Salat* : In India, the Persian term *namaaz* is more commonly used for prayers. Muslims are obliged to confirm their belief in God by remembering him five times a day. The first prayer, *fajir*, has to be said before sunrise. *Zohr* prayers are said in the early afternoon when the 'shadow of an object is equal in length to the object itself'. *Asr* prayers are recited when the sun starts turning yellow. It is time for *Maghrib* when the sun begins to set and lasts till the red disappears from the sky. *Isha* are night prayers, the final remembrance of God before the end of the day.

These prayers consist of verses from the Quran broken into units, each ending with the worshipper prostrating himself on the ground. Personal cleanliness is of utmost importance and symbolic purification, *wuzu*, is essential before the *namaaz*. The Quran also directs Muslims to face the *qibla*, the Ka'ba in Mecca, while praying. It also recommends collective praying though it can also be done individually.

Congregational prayers can be held in mosques or in any other public place and have to be led by the *imam*. However, the Quran says that any Muslim can perform the duties of the *imam*. Friday noon prayers are compulsory and one has to join the rest of the community in praying at the local mosque. The faithfuls are summoned to each prayer by the call, *adaan*, of the *muezzin*.

Fasting or *Roza* : The Muslim month of Ramadan begins with the sighting of the new moon and it is obligatory on every Muslim to fast during this period. No food or water is permitted from sunrise to sunset. The two meals during this month are the *sahri* and *iftar*, the first before the fast begins and the second is the breaking of the fast. Islam believes that fasting helps reaffirm one's faith in Allah and inculcates the principle of austerity. It also helps believers understand the sufferings of the needy. Those who are unable to fast due to ill health or other unavoidable reasons can give fixed amounts of money in charity. The month of Ramadan culminates with the sighting of the next new moon and the celebration of Id-ul-Fitr.

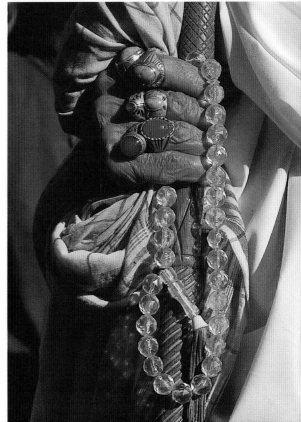

Above : A langar (free kitchen) at the shrine of a Sufi saint after an urs (festival).

Below : A faqir accepting alms in the name of god, invoking the spirit of zakaat or charity, one of the five precepts of Islam.

Previous Pages : A silhouette of the brilliantly lit Jama Masjid in Delhi, the largest mosque in India. The faithful are gathered for the evening prayer on the eve of the Eid-ul-Fitr festival.

Zakaat or Charity : It is the duty of every Muslim to donate annually, the equivalent to one-fortieth of his or her possessions including cash, jewellery, animals, agricultural and other produce. *Zakaat* emphasies the social responsibility of the Muslims towards their less fortunate brothers. Muslims believe that everything belongs to Allah and man must use them as God himself would: by sharing with those in need. The Quran insists that *zakaat* must be given only to the poor and the deserving and priorities are laid down for this: to a deserving relative, to the disabled and to the poor in that order.

48

Hajj or **Pilgrimage :** Mecca, home to the Ka'ba, is the holiest shrine of Islam. The Prophet performed the *Hajj* for the first time when he returned to Mecca from Medina after its people finally came to accept Islam. In imitation of this holy journey, all Muslims blessed with the material and physical means have to perform *Hajj* at least once in their lifetime. The pilgrimage is undertaken between the seventh and tenth day of the last lunar month of Dhul i Hijja. The *Hajj* ends with the festival of Id-al-Adha, to commemmorate Abraham's willingness to perform the greatest sacrifice demanded of a human, that of his son.

The *Hajj* stresses strong social principles. Muslims from all over come together on this occasion and worship collectively, forgetting social and racial differences. Every pilgrim dresses alike in the *ihram,* which consists of two pieces of unstitched white cloth. This shroud-like dress is supposed to remind human beings of their mortality. Men tie one cloth around their waist and drape the other over their shoulders. Women have to cover their body barring their face, hands and feet, and must be accompanied either by their husbands or other permitted male escorts.

The pilgrimage can also be performed at some other time of the year but then it is not considered *Hajj* but called *Umra.* The Quran suggests that those unable to travel themselves can pay for the *Hajj* of a poor.

Though the Quran contains the essence of Islam, Muslims are governed by guidelines provided by other sources. Nothing in these can contradict the basic message or instructions of the Quran, yet they are essential for they provide the framework within which the Muslims are supposed to live their lives. Thus the Quran lays down the basic principles and the *Sunnah,* the *Shariah* and the *Fiqh* provide specific guidance.

The *Sunnah* is the ways and practices of the Prophet. The life of Muhammad as the chosen messenger of God has always been a source of inspiration for Muslims; everything the Prophet did was considered worthy of emulation and became the ideal for individual piety.

A Sufi saying

A beggar went to a door, asking for something to be given to him. The owner answered, and said: 'I am sorry, but there is nobody in.' 'I don't want anybody,' said the beggar, 'I want food.'

Hakim Jami

Hadith or tradition is the way the *Sunnah* was preserved after Muhammad died. These traditions have forged a historical link between the Muslims and their Prophet. To prevent people from wrongly attributing facts to him, a methodology was evolved to test the genuine from the spurious. Witnesses and a chain of authorities directly linking to the Prophet had to be provided to substantiate each *Hadith* before it was accepted.

The rules governing the Muslims' lives are called *Shariah*, 'the way'. They cover all contingencies of human existence from birth to death and form an all encompassing legal system.

The need to determine the *Shariah* law in detail led to the development of *Fiqh*, the science of Islamic jurisprudence. *Fiqh* had four roots: the Quran, the *Hadith*, the *Ijma* and the *Qayas*. *Ijma*, meaning consensus, indicates the recognition by Muslims to work through commonly accepted views on contentious issues. *Qayas* is analogy or finding solutions by referring to similar situations in the *Hadith*. *Fiqh* was developed after a widespread debate within the Muslim community.

Not surprisingly, there were different historical traditions or *Hadiths* that were adopted which crystallised into four different schools or *madhab*. The differences were mainly over methodology and details. Each *madhab* came to be identified after the revered master of each school: Abu Hanfa (Hanafi), Malik bin Anas (Maliki), Al Shafi'i (Shafi'i) and Ahmad bin Hambal (Hambali). Muslims could choose any *madhab* but they tend to follow that prevalent in their region.

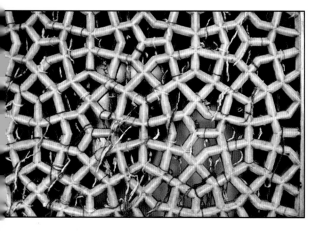

Below : *Threads tied at a Sufi shrine represent the devotees' desire to seek the intervention of the saint. On fulfillment of the wish, the devotees return to the shrine and untie the threads.*

The Ulama

The 'ulama' are not priests. In fact there is no priestly class in Islam. Any Muslim who has a thorough knowledge of the Quran and of the prescribed forms can lead the prayer, perform marriages and supervise burials.

'Ulama' is the plural of the word 'alim'. Derived from 'ilm' or knowledge, 'alim' means 'a knowledgeable one.' The early ulama were men learned in Islamic religious studies. They knew the Quran and the 'Sunnah' and helped in the evolution of the 'Shariah' in the light of Quranic ideals. They were the ones who articulated the way Muslims should live their lives.

It was only natural that these people become religious leaders. They influenced the development of Muslim law. Their voice was heard by the rulers as well as the subjects, even if they were not associated with the government.

The power of the 'ulama' as a group was consolidated during the caliphate. The state

An imam praying for the dead in a Muslim cemetery in Kelamayu in Xinjiang, China.

Below, left : Muslims shake hands with the imam and exchange greetings following a religious service.

became the patron of religion: it built and maintained mosques and 'madarsas' (religious schools). It could thus appoint the 'imam' who would lead prayers at a particular mosque or an 'alim' who supervised an educational institution. 'Imams' of larger mosques naturally developed extra-religious authority.

The state also needed the services of the 'ulama' to man the judicial system. They appointed 'alims' as 'qazis' (law givers) to maintain the state's legal system. The 'ulama' were also entrusted with the supervision of the state's charitable activities.

However all the 'ulama' were not co-opted by the state. A vast number continued to pursue knowledge inspired by faith and curiosity. It is they who wrote religious commentaries and discourses, and continued to supervise the religious education of others.

Bismillah in Tughra style, shaped like a bird speaking Arabic. Tughra is a form of pictorial and decorative calligraphy, in which the text forms the outline of an animal, a human face or a pattern.

As I think of rhymes and verses, my beloved says:
Think only of my form.
I answer: Will you not sit beside me and rejoice,
O Rhyme of my thought? . . .
Then what are these letters that they should absorb your mind, what are they?
Why, they are the thorns which surround the vine.
Yes, I shall annul the letter by means of voice and language.
And I shall hold with you a converse beyond all letters,
Beyond all voice and language.

Jalal al-Din Rumi

Sufism

Above : Simurgh, a mythical bird, is a Sufi symbol found in numerous Sufi allegories.

Facing Page : Qawwali session at a Sufi dargah (shrine) in Peshawar, Pakistan.

A sixteenth century Persian dervish with stigmata wounds.

I saw a child carrying a light.
I asked him where he had brought it from.
He put it out, and said:
'Now you tell me where it is gone.'

Hasan of Basra

Every religion has a mystical aspect and often it is this esoteric approach to God that makes religion meaningful to many people. It is an individual's quest for God's truth that gives religion its spirituality.

The spread of Islam cannot be simply seen as the ambitions of Muslim rulers. A far more effective conduit was the lives of Muslim mystics, known as Sufis. It was they who carried Islam into areas where armies never reached, touched those aspects of people's lives which were never the concerns of the *ulama*.

In Islam, mysticism is called *tasawwuf*. Though there were mystics in Islam right from its early days, Sufism is a term used for Muslim mysticism after it was organised into a movement. The term comes from the Arabic word *suf* which means wool—since the early Sufis wore coarse woollen garments to protest against the materialistic lifestyles of the prosperous Muslims, the name stuck.

Like in other religions, there emerged a section in Islam which was disillusioned with the ways of the material world. Deeply devout, they were in search of a world that was more conducive to their spiritual growth. But when they found the society at discord with their spiritual needs, they turned to mysticism. In most religions such individuals abandon their family and friends and enter monasteries or retreat to the forests. In Islam, this was not possible for it stressed the individual's responsibility to society and discouraged renunciation. Even celibacy was never encouraged in Islam. The Sufis thus lived in society and interacted with other humans. Their devotion to God and lack of concern for worldly matters were obvious to others and many were attracted by their example. The Sufis in fact had a far greater impact on society than mystics in any other religion. To many, Sufis were the true representatives of Islam, many others were introduced to Islam through the Sufis.

Early Sufis were given to devotion, piety and austerity. They believed in the Quran as the word of God and looked to it as a guide for the benefit of the soul. Since they were looking for a personal religious experience, the Sufis were unconcerned with customs, rituals and dogma. They did not question the

Devotees offering chadar (ceremonial cover) during an urs celebration.

Dancing dervishes in Istanbul, Turkey.

The Danger of Ecstasy

If a dervish remained in a state of ecstasy,

He would be fragmented in both worlds.

Saadi of Shiraz

Shariah—the unwritten law of Islam—but freed themselves from its constraints by insisting that the *Shariah* was only concerned with the external aspects of religion. Their's was an inner quest and they had to search for their own path, the *tariqah*.

The Sufis disregarded the views of the theologians and rulers and developed their own theory of piety within the framework of Islam. The purpose of Sufi devotion was the achievement of religious ecstasy. For this they found their own forms of worship. The Quran enjoins upon people to remember God—*Dhikr Allah*. The Sufis used *dhikr* or the repetition of God's name or his attributes as a meditative technique. They later added music (*sama*), poetry and dance as methods of inducing a meditative trance.

Hasan al Basri (d AD 728) is regarded as the first important Sufi saint. Another well-known Sufi was Mansur al Hallaj who was executed for uttering *ana'l haqq*—I am the truth—an act of blasphemy according to the Quran. Rabia (d AD 801) was a woman Sufi in Basrah. A slave girl who was also a musician and a poetess, there is an interesting apocryphal legend about her. She is supposed to have run through the streets of Basrah, a flame in one hand and water in the other. She said she wanted to douse the flames of hell and burn paradise so that people would love God for his own sake.

The core of the Sufi system was the relationship between the master and the pupil, the *pir* and the *murid*. The *pir* was an enlightened individual who had been successful in his search for divine truth. He had established a personal relationship with the divine and was therefore in a position to guide other seekers. The *murid* had to surrender himself spiritually to the *pir* who guided him through various stages till he reached his goal, the knowledge of God. Once the student had graduated spiritually, the *pir* appointed him as his *khalifah* (successor) and assigned him his own spiritual territory (*wilaya*) where he began guiding his own *murids*. But he continued to be in contact with his *pir*. Thus a chain was forged through which spiritual knowledge was transmitted. This chain was called the *silsillah*.

Silsillahs were usually formed around individual Sufis. Various *sillisahs* had their own interpretations of Sufism, their own network of saints and their own meditative techniques. By the twelfth century, various *silsillahs* had appeared which coexisted and respected each other's spiritual territories.

The orthodox initially frowned at Sufism and even tried to repress it. The *ulama*, the learned men of Islam, were uncomfortable with the religion of the Sufis, especially their insistence on *dhikr* as the most effective form of worship. They were also unhappy with the Sufis' casualness towards what were considered the sacred duties of every Muslim—prayers and pilgrimage. Neglecting them was an unforgivable offence in their eyes. The Sufis argued that obligatory piety was inessential for those who were constantly involved in the worship of God.

However, since the *ulama* were close to the state, the state too was often hostile to the Sufis. This conflict in the long run proved destructive for Islam as it resulted in the victimisation of some of the most pious men of the community. It was after the great Muslim thinker Imam Ghazali's (d AD 1111) campaign for the acceptance of Sufism that it came to be considered a legitimate part of Islam.

Sufi orders tended to flourish in lands far from the heartland of the caliphate—Iran, India and North Africa—and in areas which had little contact with the elite of Baghdad. In these frontier regions, the Sufis came into contact with either non-Muslims or recently converted Muslims. Preaching came naturally to these Sufis and they converted these people to their views by the sheer example of their lives. They represented an Islam that was not the product of highly intellectual debates of the *ulama* and philosophers. Besides, the Sufis spoke of Islam not in Arabic but in the language of the people.

The Sufis lived amongst people and dealt with their religious and cultural traditions with respect. They often took over causes that touched the lives of the people, even if it meant an open conflict with the state. There are instances of large groups converting en masse after their contact with a single Sufi. Entire craft guilds, for instance, attached themselves to Sufi orders.

Four major 'Silsillahs'
* *Chishti*
* *Qadiri*
* *Suhrawardi*
* *Naqshbandi*

Whoever gives advice to a heedless man is himself in need of advice.

Saadi of Shiraz

Following Pages : An aerial view of the Fatehpur Sikri near Agra in northern India. In the forefront is the impressive Jama Masjid with the marble covered shrine of Sheikh Salim Chishti, Sufi saint revered among Indians of all religions.

A Pakistani dervish.

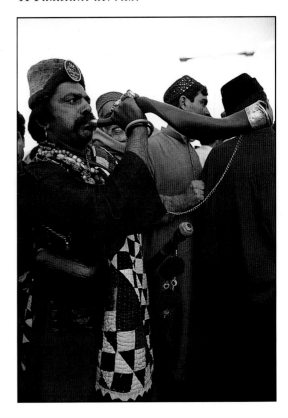

Though 'wine' is forbidden, this is
according to who drinks it,
As to how much, also with whom
it is drunk.
When these three requirements are
fulfilled; speak only—
Then, if the Wise may not drink
'wine', who should?

Omar Khayyam

*A Sufi fakir, who has given up
all his worldly possessions, lives
the life of an ascetic accepting
whatever is offered to him.*

Another reason for the large following of the Sufis was their use of music, and at times dance, as a means of achieving a state of mystical trance. Music made worship personal and meaningful to the masses. In fact, Sufi *khanqahs* (headquarters) often attracted more people than the mosques. It is from their use of music that *qawwali* and other such genres of singing evolved. Since the Sufis were free of dogmatic rigidity, they became patrons of much literary and artistic creativity. They used poetry as a means of communication—many of the leading Muslim poets were Sufis and Islamic literature benefitted greatly from mystic poetry.

The Sufis depended on alms for their survival. They were often wealthy, thanks to endowments made by wealthy disciples, which they distributed as charity. The *khanqahs* also offered hospitality to travelling Sufis and other journeymen. They were venues for regular *sama* sessions and social gatherings. People attracted to the ways of the Sufis but not willing to submit totally to the mystic discipline also attached themselves to the *khanqahs*.

With devotion around individual Sufi saints growing, their place of burial, the *dargah*, developed a special place within Sufism. The tombs of Sufi saints are the heart of a living, popular religion. The *barakka* or the grace of the saint and his spiritual powers are supposed to linger around his grave and devotees continued to beg him to intercede with God on their behalf to get their wishes fulfilled. The cenotaphs represent the continued physical presence of the saint's spiritual powers and became focuses of pilgrimage.

Devotion to *pirs* has a powerful appeal for not just Sufis but to the followers of other religions as well. People collect here the year round to supplicate or meditate. Thursday afternoons are particularly auspicious. Devouts come with offerings of *chadars* (covers for the cenotaph), flowers, incense and *nazar* (gift) for the *pirzadas*, descendents of the saint buried there. Musicians gather in the courtyard of *dargahs* and sing spiritual songs expressing the saint's passionate love for god. The poor too flock to the *dargahs* as many of them run free kitchens.

Across the subcontinent, differing rituals and offerings, charms and talismans, have become associated with various *dargahs*. The tying of a thread while praying for a wish, the untying of another string when the wish is granted, is perhaps the most popular.

Urs is the main festival associated with the *dargah*. Meaning marriage, it marks the death anniversary of the saint and is celebrated as his union with the divine beloved. *Urs* of various saints have become a regular feature of the Muslim devotional calendar. They are also the most public display of religiosity and cut across religious divides in their appeal. Pilgrims gather together on these occasions as do the *qawwals*, the practitioners of Sufi music, the *qawwali*. In some *dargahs*, the celebrations also include dance.

The Sufis began to be considered representatives of Islam and acquired a dimension that was to define the shape of Islam and the lives of peoples, both Muslims and non-Muslims.

The shrine of Hazrat Nizamuddin Auliya in Delhi, visited by numerous mureeds (devotees).

The true lover finds the light only if, like the candle, he is his own fuel, consuming himself.

Attar Nishapur

61

Bismillah calligraphed in
Tughra style takes the form of a
hawk.

He created the heavens
And the earth
In time (proportions):
He makes the Night
Overlap the Day, and the Day
Overlap the Night:
He has subjected
The sun and the moon
(To His law):
Each one follows a course
For a time appointed.

Sura XXXIX, 5

Arts and Creativity

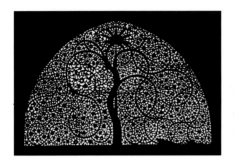

Islamic art developed over wide space and time. It started in the seventh century and continues till today. In space, it extended from Spain and Morocco in the west through Central Asia and the Indian subcontinent to Indonesia in the east. Islamic art therefore evolved from diverse artistic traditions—Arab, Irani, Berber, Turkish and Indian. Each cultural zone had its own distinct regional traditions. In India, for instance, strands of Islamic art evolved in Kashmir, the Gangetic plains, Bengal and the Deccan. There were further variations which could be identified with different classes and social groups: on the one hand were the rulers with their courts. On the other, the nomadic tribes and the common folk. Besides these, there was the urban population which included traders and craftsmen.

The Quran did not provide any regulatory directive for the artists or craftsmen, which partly explains the variations found in art from place to place and from time to time. Despite these variations, there were strong underlying principles which acted as unifying forces and which make Islamic art identifiable. These were the universal Islamic norms which governed the way of life and the attitudes of the Muslims: the strong consciousness of belonging to the *ummah*; the common purpose expressed through rituals and beliefs and most important, a common knowledge of the cosmos, of politics and of government.

The heartland of Islamic empire was one political and cultural entity for centuries together and extended its impact on Iran, India and North Africa. The most crucial factor contributing to a unified vision was the mobility of Islamic civilisation. Whole populations migrated to different lands carrying with them their aesthetic visions and traditions. The Seljuks are a good example. They moved in the eleventh century and this affected Anatolia and Iran and formed the basis of the Ottoman empire. Migrations encouraged the exchange of ideas and the cross-fertilisation is evident in all the arts.

The expanse and success of the early Islamic empire also affected the nature of Islamic art. The boundaries of the empire

Between the sixteenth and the eighteenth centuries, floral patterned ceramic tiles in turquoise, deep blue, purple, leaf green and tomato red adorned the best Ottoman buildings. This period in fact marked the golden age of Turkish ceramic art.

Facing Page : *An ornate mausoleum typical of Samarqand monuments.*

Exquisite tilework at Bibi Khanum's Mosque (above) and the Registan Square (below) in Samarqand.

included many strains which melted in the crucible of Islamic creativity. Skilled workers of varied art forms were brought together from various regions; for instance, craftsmen from Syria and Egypt built the Prophet's mosque in Medina in AD 707-09. The great Umayyad Mosque in Damascus was also built by Egyptians.

This import of skill became a feature of most Islamic sultanates. Timur's capital at Samarqand was built by craftsmen from Syria and Turkey. Similarly, the architecture of the Delhi Sultanate owed much to Muslim craftsmen who migrated to India. This was not just limited to architecture. The Mughal emperor Humayun developed a fondness for Persian miniature painting which resulted in an amalgam of Indian and Persian styles and the creation of the Indo-Islamic school of painting.

Commercial activity and the wealth of the Muslim ruling elite also made for extensive patronage of art. The *Hajj* was an important factor which brought together diverse cultures.

Calligraphy: The Arabic script is the most popular decorative motif used in Islamic art. It is found consistently all over the Islamic world from Spain to India and from the earliest to the most recent times. This can be attributed to the importance attached by Muslims to the word of God. Verses from the Quran were inscribed on many important monuments, the earliest being the Dome of the Rock in Jerusalem. This inscription is twenty-four meters long and includes verses indicating the building's function and ends with the name of the caliph and the date. Arabic calligraphy introduced a thread of unity into Islamic art: it was found even in areas where Arabic was not the spoken language. Its use symbolised the affirmation of the faith for it was addressed to God and not to man. Even the world of architecture leaned heavily on the works of great calligraphers.

Calligraphy thus became one of the most respected arts of the Islamic world and calligraphers who introduced new styles of forming and fashioning the script became more famous than any other artists. Other examples of symbolic writing are found in Muslim coinage and in the tradition of honouring distinguished people with robes of honour. These robes had the name and title of the caliph, the place of manufacture of the vestment and the date woven into them. Similar use of Arabic is found in other forms of art—metal and glass ware, carpets and textiles, paintings and so on.

Sculpture and figural arts were however not popular as statues and figures were associated with pagan idols and not approved by the Quran or the *Hadith.* In compensation, Islamic art is rich in geometric and epigraphic decorations and in landscapes. Official resistance to figural paintings weakened in the course of time and the brush acquired equal significance as the pen.

Rising to a height of seventy-three metres, the Qutb Minar in Delhi. Bands of calligraphy in Kufic script are verses from the Quran and eulogies to its patron ruler, Qutb-ud-din Aibak.

Above, left : *Tughra in the form of a tiger.*

Below, left : *The sarcophagus of Mumtaz Mahal within the Taj, inscribed with the ninety-nine names of Allah.*

Intricate calligraphy on the facade of the Taj Mahal.

Painting: Unlike calligraphy which was inspired completely by religion, Islamic painting had very little to do with it. The *ulama* were reluctant to legitimise any figural representation for this was considered idolatry and an attempt by man to mimic the Creator. Figural representations, even when popular, were never allowed to impinge on any art that had a religious connection. However, painting came to be considered as a sign of fine taste and refinement and was much valued by courtiers and merchants.

In the hey days of the caliphate, painting as an art form was patronised though it acquired definite form later. It was used more as a method of recreating geometric patterns which could be infinitely extended. But there were a few landscapes, still-lifes and even portraits.

An important feature of paintings was that they were commissioned to fit into a wider artistic scheme. Mural paintings were a part of architecture, paintings in manuscripts were not isolated entities but part of a book, all pages of which might be works of art. This art would not just consist of the paintings but would include the prose or the poetry, the calligraphy, the borders and the binding.

The graphic and visual arts of China were to have the most important impact on Islamic painting, particularly in Central Asia, Iran and the Indian subcontinent. Under the Mongols, there was an active exchange of peoples, goods and ideas and by the thirteenth and fourteenth centuries, Chinese art had been assimilated especially in western Iran and Khurasan. Chinese birds, vegetation and landscapes were incorporated into painting but they were imbued with an Islamic spirit.

Facing Page : This miniature of Babur being received by dignitaries on the banks of a river illustrates Babur's memoirs, the Babur Nama. Mughal miniature painting was inspired by Persian traditions which in itself was influenced by Chinese art.

Carried to Persia by the Mongols, elements of Chinese art were incorporated by the Muslim painters, particularly in Khurasan, Iran and Central Asia.

It was in Iran that the most vibrant developments in Islamic painting took place. It was here that painters were first given the high personal recognition that was till now reserved for calligraphers and singers. Miniature painters found in the Iranian epics ideal and abundant material for illustration. Epics like those of Laila-Majnun, Khusrau-Shireen and Yusuf-Zulaikha were enriched by the painters' interpretations of these immortal love stories. These illustrations opened up a new world of colour. The name of Bihzad stands out among the painters of Iran. Trained in Herat, he was much sought after by the great rulers of his time and under him Iranian painting scaled new heights of perfection. His style was to become the point of departure for painting from the sixteenth century.

Painters' skills were also utilised for tooling and embossing leather covers, bindings of books and to lacquer paintings which were used as book covers. These techniques were also extended to decorate other items like dishes, trays, pen cases, mirror cases and boxes of all kinds.

In India, the earliest book of illustrations dates from the reign of the independent Sultans of Malwa in the fifteenth and sixteenth centuries. But it was the Mughal emperor Humayun who was particularly interested in painting. His patronage led to the beginnings of the Indo-Islamic school of miniature painting.

The later Mughal emperors continued to be enthusiastic patrons of this art form. In 1567, Emperor Akbar ordered an illustrated copy of the *Hamza Nama*. A team of hundred painters, gilders and binders were commissioned to complete this work under the supervision of the two great Persian painters, Saiyyid Ali and Abd as Samad, products of the Bihzad school. The *Hamza Nama* was in twelve volumes, had 1004 pages and the entire enterprise took fifteen years to complete. This manuscript shows a fascinating evolution of style as the paintings towards the end of the book represent a synthesis of the Mughal and Rajput schools. Other works like the *Ramayana* and the *Mahabharata* were also translated and illustrated.

Facing Page : Portrait of Mir Mussavir by Mir Saiyyid Ali, the master painter of Mughal emperor Akbar's atelier (1565-70). The mir (nobleman) is shown reading a scroll which is in fact an application for a job. Photograph courtesy: Musee Guimet (No. 3619-1b).

71

Mughal emperor Jahangir holding a portrait of the Madonna. The painting is an exquisite example of official portraiture of the early seventeenth century.

Akbar's son Jahangir was known for his passionate interest in miniature painting and under his patronage, dynamic developments took place in this art form. For the first time, skills of individual painters came to be recognised as individual specialities. Many artists with different levels and areas of expertise worked on the same painting; one doing the faces, another the landscape, a third the gold paint and so on. Important painters of Jahangir's time included Manohar, Miskin, Govardhan and Mansur. The last was a master at painting animals and flowers. Jahangir was also interested in European art and exposed his painters to it. Elements from European, particularly Italian art were also incorporated into Mughal miniatures.

The Padshanama (Chronicle of the King of the World, written by Abdul Hamid Lahawri) has long been recognised as one of the greatest works made for the Mughal Emperor Shah Jahan, Jahangir successor and the builder of the Taj Mahal. It documents the first ten years of his rule and contains 44 magnificient illustrations and two elaborate illuminations, including works by the finest artists of the time. Among the events recorded are court ceremonies set within the splendour of Mughal architecture, hunting and battle scenes.

Some of the later volumes have been lost. However, the first three volumes which were in the possession of the royal house of Oudh since the eighteenth century were presented by the Nawab of Oudh to the Governor General of India, Lord Teignmouth, to be presented to George III, king of England. It is now part of the Royal Library at Windsor Castle.

Facing Page : A painting from the Padshahnama depicting the wedding procession of Dara Shikoh, one of the sons of the Mughal emperor Shah Jahan.

The mimbar in the mosque near the shrine of Hazrat Nizamuddin in Delhi.

The ornamental niche or mihrab at the mosque adjoining Sheikh Yusuf Qattal's tomb in Khirkee, Delhi.

Facing Page : *The gateway to Akbar's tomb in Sikandra, near Agra. The exquisite mosaics and inlays in coloured stone are of the finest Mughal craftmanship.*

Architecture : From Spain and Morocco to Samarqand and India, Islamic architecture is a museum for the history of the development of world architecture. Islamic buildings are the best examples of the synthesis of different aesthetic expressions into one larger vision. Various regional schools developed under the umbrella of Islamic building art. Each retained its distinctive feature, yet they were all united at a level which distinguishes them as Islamic, no matter where they are in the world.

The mosque is central to Islamic architecture. Though there is no one definite design—it usually reflects regional fashions—the basic concept of all mosques remains the same. They are all directed towards the Ka'ba. *Mihrab*, a real or simulated, ornamented niche in the wall facing the *qibla* is found in most mosques. It symbolically focuses the attention of the worshippers in one direction. In front of the *mihrab* stands the *imam*, the person leading the prayer. *Mimbar* is a platform to the right of the *mihrab* from where the *imam* gives religious discourses before the Friday prayer. Mosques most often have a *sahn* (courtyard) which serves an aesthetic and functional purpose. It floods light into the mosque and can accommodate large numbers for congregational prayers. The size of the courtyards vary and they are usually ornamented with paving tiles. The *sahn* also has a water tank for *wudu*, the obligatory ablutions before prayer.

Mosques are most often identified by their minarets or *minars* from where the *muezzin* makes the *adaan* (summons for the prayer). Early mosques in Spain, Iran and Iraq had square minarets. In Sammara they were spiral, reflecting an older Sassanid design. The predominant design in the Ottoman empire was the cylindrical tapering *minar*. There is no prescribed position for the *minars* nor are their numbers fixed but due to their architectural prominence and liturgical function, the minarets have acquired the significance of a symbol.

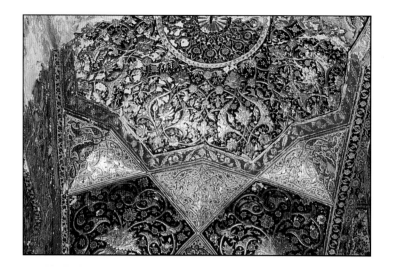

The roots of mosque architecture have been traced back to the Arabs. The word *mihrab* exists in pre-Islamic literature as does the *qubba* or dome. Pre-Islamic *qubba* was a small, domed leather tent under which the tribes kept their sacred stones. The profusion of domes and arches—the most effective way of spanning and covering large areas while still maintaining a feeling of space—are a distinctive feature of Islamic architecture which distinguish it from European, Chinese, Hindu and Buddhist architectures.

Apart from the mosques, different designs developed for mausoleums, *khanqahs*, covered markets, caravan *serais* (rest houses), public baths and palaces. Most of these monuments are from the medieval period and again, there is no single style. In some, form takes precedence over decoration while in others, it is the decoration which is the striking feature.

The architecture of Spain reflects North African and European features, the best examples being the palace at Granada and the mosque at Cordoba. Colour became the distinctive feature of Iranian architecture. The brilliance of hues was heightened by the use of ceramic tiles over large domes. Samarqand is a stunning example of this style.

India provides its own great examples of Islamic architecture. The earliest example is the impressive Qutb Minar, the beautifully decorated, five-storied, red sandstone structure. The Persian concept of the monumental tomb was imported with Humayun's tomb and reached the pinnacle of beauty in the Taj Mahal. Akbar's fortress city at Fatehpur Sikri is an interesting complex of public and private buildings. Shah Jahan was also a prolific builder and his reign was particularly fruitful as far as architectural wonders were concerned.

A pierced stone window from Sidi Sayid's mosque in Ahmedabad in western India. Built in 1572, the intricate carving and ornamental relief work are inimitable in style and skill.

Above, left : *Detail of the ornately painted and inlaid ceiling of Akbar's tomb in Sikandra.*

The Gol Gumbaz, built by
Sultan Muhammad of
Bijapur, a descendent of the
Turkish Adil Shahi dynasty.
The dome is almost as large as
that of the Pantheon or St.
Peter's Cathedral in Rome.

Overleaf : *View of the Taj
Mahal from the Fort of Agra.*

*Entrance to the imposing
Lahore Fort.*

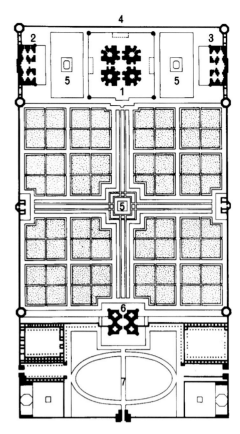

Gardens: Linked to the concept of heaven, gardens were also of primary importance in Islamic architecture. They are often cited as symbols of paradise with shade and water as ideal elements. The Quran frequently mentions 'gardens' with rivers flowing below them. The four rivers of paradise are believed to be that of water, milk, wine and purified honey.

This description probably gave rise to the *charbagh* or the quartered garden. Originating in Iran, they were divided by four water channels within a walled enclosure. Islamic gardens were formally planned with geometrically laid-out paths, flower beds and water courses within which houses, palaces and mausoleums were set. This layout was a response to the arid and featureless monotony of the surrounding desert. Gardens described in poetry were also recreated on tiles, mosaics, ceramics and on carpets. Gradually, these gardens became status symbols of the rich and the powerful. They soon led to landscaped architecture of great beauty in Persia and the beauty of these planned gardens had an influence on the decorative arts.

Site plan and view of the Taj Mahal showing the charbagh— a quartered garden typified in the Hasht Bahist of Isfahan (literally eight paradises).

Facing Page : *A fountain in Alhambra Palace, Spain.*

A muezzin at the Jama Masjid, Delhi, calling the faithful to prayer.

Music : Whether music is permissible to Muslims or not is an old and futile debate because the Quran provides no specific verdict on the subject. The earliest critics were clearly against music which had come to be associated with liquor and debauchery and with the luxurious lifestyle of the rich. Be that as it may, music began in the very first century of Islam for there was never ever any debate about the *adaan*, the prayer call from the mosque. Muhammad had himself established this tradition between AD 622-624. The first *muezzin* was the freed slave Bilal, whose martyrdom has become a matter of legend. Bilal was also the patron saint of the *muezzin* guilds in Turkey and Africa.

The *adaan* consists of twelve musical phrases and a seven-line text. Its structure is formed by the phrasing of the text and its repetition. The melody varies and reflects regional musical styles. The *adaan* is intoned five times a day by someone with a powerful and expressive voice. The Quran is also chanted in unornamented musical styles at varying rhythms. Rules were gradually codified regarding punctuation, accentuation and assimilation of certain letters.

Music came to be used in certain areas on special occasions like Ramadan or the birth anniversary of the Prophet. But it was the Sufis who made music an intrinsic form of worship. *Dhikr*, the Sufi method of prayer, used musical phrases and rhythms to enhance the effect of the words. This developed into full-fledged musical expressions which sometimes included dancing. Musical sessions (*sama*) at Sufi establishments became increasingly popular and across the Islamic world, many forms of musical instruments and styles emerged from these sessions.

Below : Ud, a popular Islamic instrument, and **(below, right)** an ud-player.

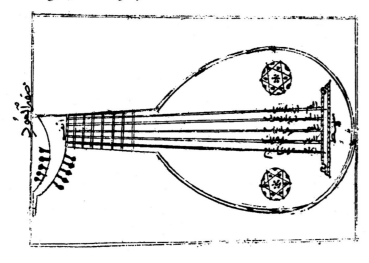

They lighted, tied their chargers to a rock,
And cautiously advanced in mail and casque
With troubled hearts.
They wrestled like two lions
Until their bodies ran with sweat and blood.
From sunrise till the shadows grew they strove
Until Suhrab, that maddened Elephant,
Reached out, up-leaping with a lion's spring,
Caught Rustum's girdle, tugged amain as though,
Thou wouldst have said, to rend the earth, and shouting
With rage and vengeance hurled him to the ground.

(From Firdausi's Shahinshah-nama, translated by Arthur and Edmond Warner)

Literature: Islamic society held in high esteem a well-developed literary taste. In fact, elegant speech and facility with words were and remain a much admired social asset. Verse occupied a far more important position than prose in Muslim literary tradition. The two most important Islamic languages, Arabic and Persian, are both extremely poetic.

The Quran was the first literary work in Arabic and considered inimitable in form and content. Its significance lay not just in the influence it had but also in its thought and literary style. Since it was divine revelation, the Quran was above criticism and could not be imitated by humans. Yet it was so fundamental to Islamic thought that it was constantly quoted and its phraseology, rhythms and style penetrated Arabic literature deeply.

The concept of *adab* was very crucial to Arabic literature. These are the unbreachable moral, social and cultural rules of conduct. Arabic literature therefore tended to have a didactic character. One of the extremely sophisticated literary genres was the *maqumat* or the assemblies. These were conversations between one witty person and a series of others. Works were seldom composed for mere entertainment; the *Thousand and One Nights* was not treated as serious literature.

Romances and love stories were extremely popular in the Islamic lands. They followed conventional patterns and usually ended in tragedies, like the story of two lovers united by the tree that grew between their graves. Laila-Majnun was undoubtedly the most popular romantic story and was translated into Persian and transmitted further into India. Animal fables designed to inculcate morals in the masses as well as regale them were among the oldest genres of Arabic literature.

Persian, the other Islamic language, emerged around AD 1000 in Iran. A combination of Arabic and Pahlavi, it became the literary language of Iran and later, India. The *Shahinshah-nama (The Story of Kings)* of Firdausi from the eleventh century is the foremost Persian classic. *The Treasury of Secrets* by Nizami, written in AD 1175, are sermons illustrated by stories.

Science: The early Muslims were very keen on scientific enquiry. Their intellectual quest was sparked and encouraged by the concerted translations into Arabic of works in Greek, Persian, Syriac, Hebrew and Indian languages. This amazing gathering of writings gave a great fillip to intellectual and rational thought among the Muslims. Muslim rulers patronised scholars as enthusiastically as they patronised poets or other artists. There was a craze for scientific novelties at the Islamic courts and the rulers were surrounded by astrologers and physicians.

Muslims all over the world were also very keen on scientific instruments and mathematicians could astronomically determine and define the times of prayer and the direction of Mecca.

Baghdad, in the hey day of the Abbasids, became the center for science. Scholars from different nations, of different religions and speaking different languages authored scientific material in Arabic. Though sciences like mathematics, astronomy, medicine and astrology were often considered a threat to religion by some Muslims, science and philosophy continued to thrive and develop in Islamic societies for many centuries.

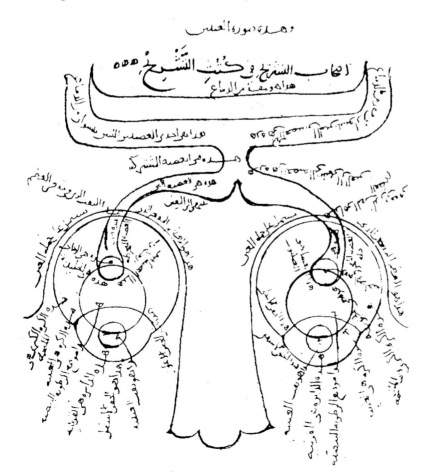

Ibn al-Haytham's volume, Optics, written in eleventh century Egypt, contained a theory of vision that went beyond the theories of Galen and Ptolemy. This diagram from a copy of the book shows the optic nerves connecting the eyeballs to the brain.

Crafts: The splendour of Islamic empires was created by the fusion of the arts and skills of the many people who came to be included in these empires. The elite were generous patrons and a system for discovery and training of talent was created.

Exhibits of Islamic art across the museums of the world show an amazing variety. Textile production was an important urban industry in the Islamic world. They provided not just clothing but tents, curtains, beddings, couches, pillows, rugs, carpets, canopies and awnings. The best example of textile are the carpets or knotted rugs, said to have been introduced by the Turkish tribes. Wollen threads were added to the flat woven fabric to provide additional thickness and these were used as floor-coverings in tents. Islamic rugs were patterned with abstract as well as floral and pictorial designs and their unique feature was the striking colour scheme—ivory white ground with deep blue and red patterns.

Inlay, moulding and carving produced millions of exquisite pieces of jewellery. Chandeliers of cutglass hung on gold chains were often found in courts and homes. Glass was painted, embossed, etched, and inlaid with gems.

The armour used by the kings and generals was also paid a lot of attention—swords, daggers, spears, shields and helmets were engraved, embossed, gilded, lacquered and even studded with precious stones. Art techniques were imported from Europe and incorporated into various styles.

A gold coin from the time of Akbar, minted at Agra.

The navratan (nine-gemmed) necklace crafted during the reign of Shah Jahan.

The Shikargah brocades were inspired by Persian and Mughal miniature paintings which featured elaborate hunting scenes. Preferred by the Mughal royalty, the weavers of Banaras, a town in northern India, incorporated these into their design palette.

Termed cartouche, calligraphy is often used to decorate the ends of Persian carpets.

A carpet dealer with his son in north west Peshawar.

Craftsmen embroidering the popular Islamic symbol, Ul Burraq, on a silk carpet to be used during Muharram.

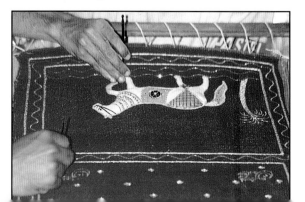

A mosaic of fine tile inlay at Chini ka Rauza in Agra. Built in 1639, the outside walls of this tomb are decorated with these tiles which show a distinct Persian influence.

A panel from the famed Jamewar shawl. This complex weave originated in Kanishma, a small village in the Kashmir valley in India, and was introduced into Turkey in the first half of the nineteenth century

Pietra dura, a technique believed to have originated in Italy, was used lavishly on the Taj Mahal. In this style, designs are carved into marble and inlaid with jasper, agate, carnelian, bloodstone, lapis lazuli and other precious and semi-precious stones.

An intricately etched and silver-inlaid metalware from Moradabad. Patronised by the Mughals, this art was traditionally in the hands of Muslim artisans.

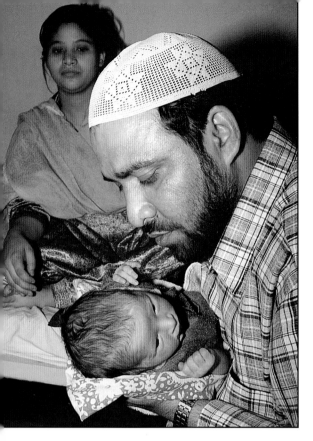

The adaan being recited in the ear of a newborn to initiate him into Islam.

A Bismillah ceremony where the elder initiates the child into reading.

Rites of Passage

Islam prescribes five essential rites which are a must for all Muslims. These rites are governed by the *Sunnah* or the 'Established Practices'.

Birth: Soon after birth, the *adaan* comprising verses of the Quran is whispered into the newborn's ears. Since the words entering the child's ears are the words of God, the *adaan* marks the child's initiation into Islam. The ritual can be performed by any Muslim as Islam does not have priests. Circumcision is another compulsory ritual for all male Muslims.

Naming Ceremony: The newborn acquires a name formally after its head is shaved and a goat or a sheep sacrificed. The flesh of these animals is distributed, along with the weight of the shaved hair in silver, among the poor.

Bism Allah: A common ceremony, particularly in India, this literally means 'I begin in the name of Allah'. When a child turns five, he is initiated into his obligatory duties when he repeats with an adult, a verse from the Quran. It is the duty of every parent to teach their children to read the Quran and to perform their prayers. After attaining puberty, every person is himself or herself responsible for performing the prescribed obligations.

Marriage: At the base of the Islamic social structure is the family. The Quran considers the nuclear family—husband, wife and children— as a self sufficient social unit. A man is permitted to marry four times, but only under specific conditions and with the permission of the earlier wife or wives. Each of these marriages has the same status and the responsibility of maintaining the children is the father's.

Islamic marriage is a contract between a consenting man and a consenting woman. Although most marriages are arranged by the elders, the concerned couple are consulted and never coerced. In the formal ceremony called *nikah*, each partner is asked if he is willing to enter into marriage with the other. If they agree, the contract is sealed by declaration and consent in the presence of two witnesses. The man also has to give *mehr* (an assurity in money) to his wife at the time of marriage. This is to protect her rights in case of divorce which is permitted by the Quran.

Muslims are allowed to marry a member of the 'People of the Book'. They can also marry their paternal and maternal cousins and cousins of parents. But marrying a foster parent, parents or siblings is taboo. Two sisters also cannot be married to the same man simultaneously.

Celebration of marriage and associated customs vary from society to society. There is no prescribed celebration except the declaration of marriage by man with a feast.

Death: Muslims believe that uttering the word of God in a dying man's ears helps the soul reach heaven. After death, the body is purified by a bath. There is a prescribed procedure laid down which must be strictly followed. For instance, it can only be performed by a close kin of the same sex as the deceased. After the bath, the body is shrouded in a *kafan* which consists of three pieces of unstitched white cloth. There is a congregational prayer for the dead before burial.

The nikaah of Nawab Abdul Mazid Khan of Savanur with Nawabzadi Anjum Sultana of Balasinor. In traditional Islamic weddings, the bride is segregated from the groom until after the contract has been signed in the presence of two witnesses.

Overleaf : Nawab of Rampur Kazim Ali Khan blessing the couple after the nikaah.

The gravestones of Itmad-ud-Daula, father-in-law and prime minister of Jahangir, and his wife Asmat Begum.

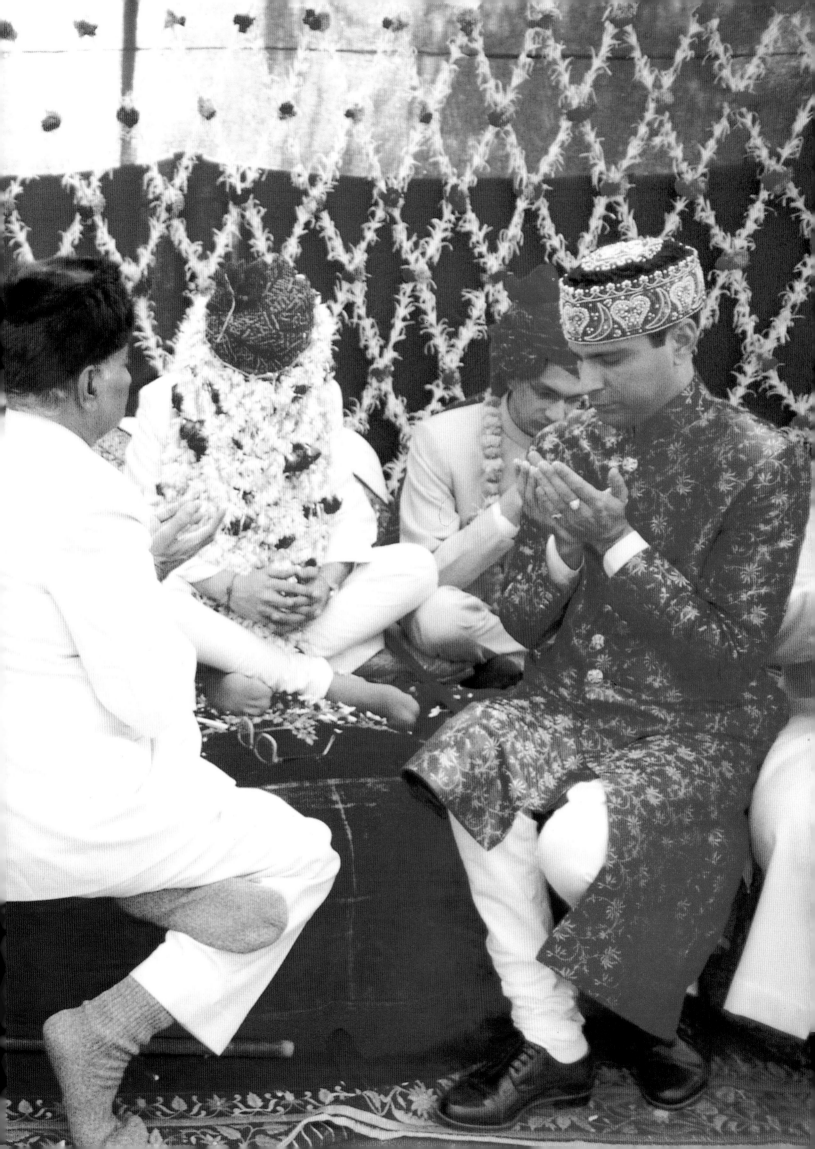

The Calendar and its Landmarks

The twelve months of the Muslim calendar are:

- *Muharram*
- *Safar*
- *Rabi ul Awwal*
- *Rabi us Sani*
- *Jumadi ul Awwal*
- *Jamadi us Sani*
- *Rajab*
- *Sha'ban*
- *Ramadan*
- *Rawwal*
- *Dhul i Qa'dah*
- *Dhul i Hijja*

The Eid bazaar outside the Jama Masjid. This historic bazaar has become a part of Delhi's history attracting Muslims and non-Muslims .

The Islamic calendar and the Hijri era began in AD 622 when Muhammad and his followers migrated from Mecca to Medina. The Islamic calender is governed by lunar movements. It consists of twelve months which correspond to twelve periods between one new moon and the next. Each month begins with the actual sighting of the new moon, so the same month might have twenty-nine or thirty days in different years and in different places. The lunar year is eleven days shorter than the solar year and the Islamic century is three years short of a solar century.

Muharram: It was in this month in AD 680 that Husayn, the son of Ali and Fatima, and grandson of the Prophet, confronted Yazid of the Umayyad dynasty. Though he and his small group of supporters were defeated, Husayn refused to surrender and was killed along with his sons Ali Asghar, Ali Akbar and Abbas.

This dramatic martyrdom of the Prophet's descendents and the anguish it generated still inspires the Muslims. To this day the event is commemorated by mourning in the first ten days of Muharram. Tales of Husayn's martyrdom are related at gatherings in both prose and poetry (*marsiya*). The mourning ends on the tenth day with a procession of *taziyas* (replicas of mausoleums) which are later buried. These processions are extremely popular in India.

Rabi ul Awwal: Prophet Muhammad is believed to have been born on the twelfth day of this month. He also died on the same date. The Prophet's birthday is celebrated with a *mawalid*. The *mawalid* or *milad* found its ritual form in northern Mesopotamia around the beginning of the thirteenth century and was soon adopted by Muslims all over the world. On this day, Muslims gather to listen to orations about the life and work of the Prophet. Verses extolling the Prophet are also sung.

Rajab: On the twenty-seventh day of this month the Prophet had a dream vision in which he visited heaven. This day is remembered as the day of *Mi'raj.*

Ramadan: The Quran is believed to have been revealed in the last week of this month. The holiest period in the Muslim calendar, it is the month when Muslims are obligated to fast, going without food and water from sunrise to sunset.

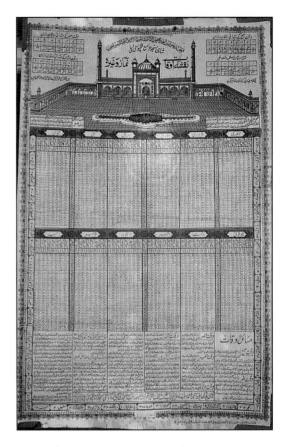

Shawwal: On sighting the new moon at the end of Ramadan, the first day of Shawwal is celebrated as Eid-ul-Fitr, a celebration which follows the fulfillment of fasting in Ramadan. On the morning of this day, Muslims join a congregational prayer of thanksgiving.

Dhul i Hijja: This is the month of Muslim pilgrimage or the *Hajj*. Performed on the eighth, ninth and tenth of this month it involves visits to Mecca, Arafat and Minnah. It concludes with a sacrifice to commemorate Abraham's readiness to give up his son for Allah. Even those Muslims who do not go on a pilgrimage celebrate the tenth day of this month by offering sacrifices and joining in community prayers ❖

An Islamic and Roman calendar combined in one, giving the time for prayers.

A souvenir shop selling clocks adorned with various Islamic icons and scriptures.

Last Page : Every Muslim looks out eagerly for a glimpse of the hilal (crescent) as it announces the beginning of the holy month of Ramadan.

Overleaf : A taziya (symbolic mausoleum) being taken round the streets of Morvi, a small town in western India, during Muharram.